SL.....
DAYS AND
BOTTLED
PYRAMIDS

If you enjoy reading this book, please consider reviewing it on Amazon, or elsewhere.

David Barto

SLATE DAYS AND BOTTLED PYRAMIDS

GROWING UP IN THE 50s AND 60s

DAVID R ROBERTS

With drawings by Anne Roberts

The Book Guild Ltd

First published in Great Britain in 2022 by
The Book Guild Ltd
Unit E2 Airfield Business Park,
Harrison Road, Market Harborough,
Leicestershire. LE16 7UL
Tel: 0116 2792299
www.bookguild.co.uk
Email: info@bookguild.co.uk
Twitter: @bookguild

Typeset in 11pt Minion Pro

Printed and bound in Great Britain by 4edge Limited
Drawings by Anne Roberts

ISBN 978 1915352 156

British Library Cataloguing in Publication Data.
A catalogue record for this book is available from the British Library.

To my parents Joan (1923–2003) and Ray (1922–1991)

Contents

Foreword

When the wind drives the rain sideways in thin horizontal sheets of piercing grey, re-stinging the chapped thighs of a 1950s childhood, these are the slate days. They are the long, ceaseless, wet and wintery Welsh quarry days of damp buses; the unrelenting boredom of a seven-year-old denied the opportunities for independent action. Everlasting days of unbroken sunshine and pure happiness. Days of meadowsweet and buttercups and infinite possibility. Days of hope as high as those magnificent three-dimensional Egyptian triangles in the big red *Book of Knowledge* which he keeps in his bedroom.

Both are preserved – like the sliced and salted runner beans in the large, glass sweet jars labelled 1955 and stored in the pantry. The outwardly drab austerity of post-war existence and the delicate but protected shoots of boundless energy and sky's-the-limit potential of the years to come – they're both still there, still clear. One looks over the shoulder at the grim realities of the second global conflagration of the first half of the twentieth century and the frozen, trapped lives of a depressed inter-war country. The other points forwards, to the culturally explosive decade of his teenage years.

These are the times before the world is blown off-course and onto the chute to self-destruction, a destination which half a century on will appear all too close. They are the times before possibility is sold off to the highest bidder, before visions of what can be turn into memories of what might have been.

Hope is a belief in a better place and is hard to destroy. The revival of young hope in recent years suggests an escape channel can still be built. In helping to reclaim the possible, perhaps the recollections of older generations – bitter and sweet, blithe or sorrowful – can contribute to its construction.

A note on names

In some places I have altered names (or other details) to avoid possible embarrassment to those concerned or to their families.

Part 1

1950s Childhood

Perfect Happiness

You're two years old and stuffing the pockets of your pale-green dungarees with warm stones and dirt on a sunny day. Bliss.

Wretched

I've been plonked on the pale pine kitchen table while my Mum and my Nan have an argument. My blue-sandalled feet and lower legs dangle over the edge and I'm wearing my favourite blue-and-white striped sun suit with the straps.

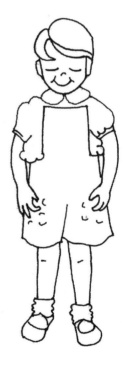

It seems they are shouting at each other about who should do their shift at Loach's shop in Greyfriars today. (They job-share, although I don't think the term has yet been invented.) They are both saying they will go. Maybe they both prefer working at the greengrocer's to looking after me.

It is the first time I see mother having one of her histrionic fits. It involves lying on the floor banging her fists and making wailing noises. I don't like it and I wail in sympathy.

There's not much room in the small kitchen for this sort of behaviour.

Ups and Downs of Tricycle Ownership

The brand-new sky-blue tricycle is possibly my first self-propelled means of personal transport, that's if you discount my red pedal car. If you count the car, then the trike is the second – but much faster. The handlebars bend inwards and terminate at the black handgrips. At the rear, beneath the saddle, there's a commodious boot that could easily accommodate sandwiches and a bottle of pop should I ever decide to run – or cycle – away from home. I'm less keen, though, on the extendable steel rod, with a third handgrip, that folds away neatly beneath the boot. Potentially this contraption affords too much parental control over speed and even direction.

Perhaps in order to attain some independence, I prefer to ride on the blind side of the house. This is the side that, strangely, has no windows. It always looks like it should have another house joined to it. But it does mean I can ride up and down the driveway, and put mud and things into the boot, without prying adult eyes.

This does have its downside though, as I discover when somehow I manage to trap my right foot between the chain wheel and its arm. I think the buckle of my red sandal is implicated too. But whatever the cause, I can't free myself. The more I struggle the firmer I'm wedged and the more my foot hurts as well. Any slight forwards movement also shifts the chain-set and increases the pain. There's barely any scope for rolling backward as I'm very close to the house wall, and in any case it doesn't seem to help.

I shout for help. No response. I try again – many times and with each shout louder and more frantic than its predecessor. I could be here all day. What about my dinner? More desperate measures are called for. With gritted milk teeth, I try a tug. It's painful but I think I detect a slight shift in my foot's position. Perhaps one – just one – very big tug will free it completely. It'll hurt a lot but, if successful, it'll be worth it. OK then. Now! …I don't recall experiencing pain like that before (but I am in only my third year of life) – and I know immediately it hasn't worked. I can't see properly if my foot is bleeding: the tears are getting in the way. I revert to the shouting method.

I think it's our next-door neighbour, Mr Bristow, who has raised the alarm. The cavalry of parents and grandparent arrive and my foot and I are liberated. It happens quite quickly – apparently a combination of skilful manoeuvring and Vaseline.

Unwanted Visitors Cause Chaos

I'm three, possibly just four years old and sitting on the back doorstep of my Nan's house. This is where I live with my parents and my Nan. Dad has left for work in the family car, which he uses for his job as a Colgate-Palmolive sales rep. He travels around the Midlands with tiny tubes of toothpaste and little bars of green soap to attract orders from corner shops and village stores. Mum is probably at work at the greengrocer's. Nan will be listening to *Housewives' Choice* on the Light Programme while vacuuming the carpet.

I'm about to call for my cousin John, who lives round the corner in Oxford Gardens, but first I have to adjust my six-shooter and holster to the correct position on my right hip. Looking up, I freeze. There's an enormous head just a few feet away. Its expression is as terrified as I am – wide-eyed and flaring nostrils – but I'm very small and the head is huge.

I turn to re-enter the house, but the door is shut behind me. I'm not tall enough for my fingers to grasp the doorknob sufficiently to turn it. I bang on the door repeatedly but the wireless and the Hoover drown my desperate cries of, "There's a cow at the back door." The cow is black and white and massive and no doubt panicking as it breaks into a sort of lumbering run towards the back lawn, destroying flowers, shrubs and sections of fence in the process.

Giving me a chance to escape, I start to run in the opposite direction along the narrow side path towards the front of the house. Ahead, another cow suddenly emerges, and another – and I'm pinned to the wall as the frightened animals run past me. More are in the front garden. The only way is back down the path towards the rear garden. Even more here. At least two are tussling with the hedge and breaking down the fence at the end of the garden. Others have already clambered through and into the neighbour's vegetable patch where Mrs Nadin is waving both arms, frantically trying to shoo them away. In the chaos, I'm sure I catch sight of one unperturbed creature bovinely munching away in the centre of our lawn.

But I also become aware of another presence in the back garden. There's a worried-looking man with a stick vainly trying to round up his charges, but he seems to be making things worse. By now, an equally anxious grandmother quickly takes in the scene through the dining room window. She runs out, gathers me up and I'm carried to indoor safety.

It turns out that the man in the garden is from the farm at the top of the road, and he'd been supervising the herd on its final on-hoof journey – to the abattoir. Passing our house, perhaps some of its members had made an escape

4

bid. More likely, they just fancied a detour and a bite to eat en route.

That evening, I listen as father receives an almighty bollocking from his mother-in-law for leaving the driveway gates open.

Incommoding Passers-by

One of my first two friends is Karol, who lives a couple of houses away up the road. Karol has eczema and asthma and a rusty old tricycle. Sometimes we hide behind the front wall of my house and chuck things over when we hear people passing. One day we manage to throw his tricycle over the wall.

Beating Hearts

There are two hearts in a Pyrex jug in permanent residence on Nan's kitchen window-sill. If I let my imagination off its lead for a bit, I can even see them beating. Sometimes I like to think that when everyone in the house has gone to bed, they talk to each other, perhaps hatching escape plans. Unlike other cuts of meat, the internal organs of butchered animals are not on ration so we often have sheep hearts for dinner. Stuffed, cooked and sliced laterally, I like them. Dad thinks they're offally good.

The Tooth, the Yoke and the Blacksmith

I like going to the village where my great-granny and some aunts and uncles live. With her long black dress, woollen shawl and bonnet and one large tooth, great gran can look a bit frightening until I get used to seeing her again. When she smiles at me the tooth gets even longer and her wrinkles look like a potato field. Her garden has all kinds of tall flowers and narrow paths lead to lots of secret places.

Uncle Albert, who is my Nan's brother, also lives in the cottage. Sometimes he takes me to the place where they milk the cows. He puts this wooden thing on his shoulders. It's called a yoke, and he uses it to carry pails of milk just like the men with white beards in old photographs. Today Uncle Albert is helping a man in a smithy. They're both wearing black leather aprons and have hammers. It's noisy and smoky but it's warm and smells better than the cowshed.

Listen Without Mother

Mum switches on the wireless and tunes it to the Light Programme. Following the tinkly piano music, the lady talks for a bit and then says: "After the music Daphne Oxenford will be here to speak to you." This is the sign for my mother to exit the room, as I prefer to listen to my daily dose of *Listen With Mother* without interruptions.

"Are you sitting comfortably?" Daphne asks me.

"Yes," I reply, wriggling into position on the pouffe to make sure I am.

"Then I'll begin." In her pruned tones Daphne then enunciates her way through the daily story before the other presenter starts on the song of the day. It's OK if mum returns at this stage, as the story is always the best bit. On the days she's not out at work she normally listens to the *Woman's Hour* programme that follows at two o'clock. Sometimes there's a police message first when you're asked to ring Whitehall 1212 if you have any information. We don't have a phone at Nan's house so I suppose we'd have to find one of those red boxes with windows. But we never have anything to tell them anyway.

Visiting the Cemetery

I like cemeteries and graveyards. Once a fortnight I go with my Mum and Nan to visit the grandfather who died five years before I was born. The cemetery entrance is off a loud road but as soon as I go through the high, heavy wrought-iron gates, there's a stillness.

My job is to take the older dead flowers and to place them on top of all the others in the large square cage-like basket. There's a water tap next to it and sometimes I also empty the vase with holes in the top and refill it.

Grandfather's grave has a grey headstone with gold lettering and in front there are chippings of a lighter grey. Some of the other graves have more brightly coloured chippings, green or blue, and some are white. These are all fascinating and I change my mind each time about which is my favourite.

Occasionally there are people at a nearby plot who look serious before bowing their heads, putting their hands together and mumbling things to themselves. I'm told in whispers that they are praying, but there are no prayers at our grave.

One of the best parts of the visit is still to come. After fresh flowers are placed in the holes at the top of the vase, we follow the bending path up a small hill to a footbridge. The bridge is over a railway line and we might be lucky to hear and then see a train approaching. If I stand on the bridge as the train puffs its way under, sometimes the engine driver will blow the whistle.

The bridge takes us to an older part of the cemetery. There are no bright chippings here and the headstones are grimier and lean at peculiar angles. The trees are bigger and there are lots of darker, shady places. Nan says there's a great aunt buried somewhere, but we never find her.

Then it's time to head back for the long walk home. As we walk out through the high gates the tranquillity is broken.

There's Been An Accident

There's a group of us who ride our tricycles down the hill of the unused bit of road by Beaconside. We can pick up a fair bit of speed before applying our brakes as we approach the bottom. Pete's trike is very old and parts of it don't always work well. Today it's the brake. As the rest of us slow to a stop before the junction with the Sandon Road, Pete doesn't. We stare as a large lorry on the main road looks set to pass the spot our friend is hurtling towards. An awful meeting of the two is seeming inevitable until suddenly Pete and his trike part company. Pete is momentarily airborne before landing horizontally – his lower half on the pitted surface of the old road, head and upper body among the overgrown verge to the left. The tricycle, on the other hand, continues on its way before temporarily disappearing under the locked wheels of the braking lorry as it slides past.

Pete's OK. One knee is grazed, the other is starting to bleed, but he's worried about his trike. A woman rushes across from the house on the corner. She says she'll take Pete inside to see to his wounds and he asks us to look after his trike. Remarkably it's still more or less in one piece – but it's very, very flat. We decide to take it back to his house.

"Hello Mrs Pete. There's been an accident and we've brought his trike back." We thought she'd be pleased. Instead, her hands jerk to her face and there's a frightful shrieking sort of noise that lasts a long time. It's a while before she understands what we're trying to tell her. She then runs off in the direction of the house on the corner.

The Daily Orange Juice Race

Mum collects it together with the cod liver oil from the dark old welfare building in Mount Street. It's free and comes in interestingly shaped bottles. Each evening Mum puts some in a glass with water. Dad then adds two straws to the glass – his and mine – and challenges me to a race. I'm not sure if it's to see who finishes first or who drinks the most, but I always win it seems.

The Wolf of Badenoch

I think my parents are trying to prepare me for school. Each evening after dad gets home from work he and mum sit on the settee with me between them. They ask which book I want to look at today. There aren't many to choose from but that doesn't matter because they're all my favourites in different ways. And anyway I like this time of day. It's cosy and warm with the three of us huddled close together and sometimes the fire is lit. I feel happy as we turn the pages, see the pictures and say the words.

On the cover of my newest book are yellow and black drawings of elves and imps and things, some I'm not that keen on. But inside are letters and words which my parents read aloud and some more drawings. Some of the pictures have words underneath and I get to recognise these after a while. One of the other books is about a nodding wooden boy-toy with a bell on his blue hat and his friend, called Big Ears, who looks a lot older and has a pointy red hat. Big Ears is the clever one whom Noddy relies on for advice. When they start to build a house, Noddy asks if they can put the roof on first in case it rains. It's a good joke because I know this isn't possible until there are walls to support it. But Big Ears looks at Noddy as if to say, 'That's stupid.'

Noddy lives in Toyland and there's a picture of it as soon as you open the front cover of the book. I'm fond of this picture because of the overlapping hills at the edge of the town which seem to shelter it, keeping it safe and secure – like I feel with my mum and dad seated each side of me. But the final book I like to look at before bedtime is the very first one I was given. It's large and has very thick, stiff cardboard pages. Each one has a picture of a steam locomotive. The best one by far is called *The Wolf of Badenoch*, but why such a splendid engine in all its powerful, frightening magnificence should be named after a notorious fourteenth-century Scottish land racketeer, plunderer, murderer and arsonist, is a question it doesn't occur to me to ask. I love the sound of the name, though; it reminds me of the Big Bad Wolf, alluring yet dangerous – like the railway engine itself. I do now know the words when I see them beneath the picture. Does this mean I'm learning to read?

Ada

Monday is normally the only day of the week when neighbours don't drop round for elevenses, but we're having more than our share of visitors today. They're very interested in something that's about to happen in the room that's in a sort of outhouse behind the coal store.

It's where Mum and Nan do the weekly wash. There's a deep white sink in one corner attached to which is a wooden draining board. Beneath the little window is an electrically powered Burco boiler out of which come great clouds of steam each time it's opened to poke and turn its contents with a large pair of wooden tongs. Clothes which can't be boiled are normally washed in the adjacent dolly tub, some of them also receiving a brutal scrubbing against a washboard from Nan's powerful forearm. After a time the tongs are employed again to lift out the clean items into the sink. From there they get their first feed through the green and red mangle. The big wooden rollers squeeze out the soapy water prior to the rinsing and more mangling.

It gets very hot in the little room with all this going on, so it's not a bad place to be in winter. I like the clean smells as well, and I'm also taken with the little bags of blue dye that are added to the washing. Mum says it's to make the whites whiter. How does that work, then?

By the end of the day's washing the window is completely steamed-up, and there's water dripping down the dark green walls and onto the red-tiled floor. So it's now mopping-up time, which I don't think Nan likes doing. When it's too cold or wet to hang the damp clothes on the back-garden washing line, she lowers the rack from the ceiling to dry the clothes inside. But she grumbles that this takes too long due to all the condensation. She's therefore made a decision and taken delivery of a brand new addition to our laundry equipment.

And this is why people keep calling round today. They want to see Ada in operation. Ada is the name of the top-loading, single-tub, wringer-type washing machine, or at least that's the description that Nan reads out to us. Apparently, it's the first in our part of the road, which accounts for the neighbourhood curiosity. I don't think Nan minds showing off her new contraption, but I suspect she'll be on the lookout for any hopeful bods bearing bundles of dirty laundry.

The machine, though, is something of a monstrosity. Its cream-coloured dimensions occupy a considerable proportion of the available floorspace, so the mangle and the dolly tub get the boot. They're now lying forlornly 'twixt dustbin and pigbin awaiting collection by the rag-and-bone man.

Old Tom and His Horse

At our house my Nan has logs for the fire delivered by Old Tom. He brings them by horse and cart. The wooden cart is a faded and worn blue. The horse waits patiently in the driveway while Tom unloads the logs and stacks them neatly against the walls of the asbestos garage – some on the inside and some outside.

The arrival of the horse triggers interest among the neighbours who usually appear with shovels. I'm told it's for their roses and rhubarb. Dad says he doesn't understand the latter – he prefers custard with his. Mum pulls a face and says Dad thinks he's a comic.

The Infinite Garden

It can get confusing at times, this business of aunts and uncles. On the one hand, we're told that they are the brothers and sisters of your parents, but could just be married to them. And then there are the older ones who turn out to be brothers and sisters of my grandparents but whom we also call uncle or aunt, although apparently they are actually great uncles or aunts – or maybe just married to them. There are lots and lots of them; I lose track. On the other hand, there's a bunch of other people I refer to as aunt or uncle who aren't related to anyone in my family. It seems that any adult living next door automatically assumes the title – and sometimes they can even be from a few doors away. My Nan is called Auntie Bo by virtually every kid in the street. Finally, close friends of my mum – Sheila, Stella, Vi – have always been my aunts. Interestingly, though, their husbands (where that applies) aren't my 'uncles' and nor are any of Dad's male friends.

This is all by way of introduction to Aunt Stella – or, more precisely, to where she lives. It's a large flat in a very large old house. The house is sort of sideways on to the gravel driveway and close to where three roads meet. What's so special about this place is the garden. It's why I love going there. To the left of the enormous front door is the start of a neatly lawned area big enough for more than a decent kick around. Sometimes there is a St Bernard dog which I'm allowed to ride for a minute or two. It doesn't appear to mind and seems gentle. There are borders to three sides of the lawn with lots of flowers. At the far end, where the flowers are taller, there's a gap which takes you into a further grassed area, but this one is different. Some of the grass is left to grow higher, so it's more feathery and a different colour at the top although there are short green winding pathways that lead to a wooden archway made from old tree branches.

If you walk through, you enter a garden divided into patches and rows of different kinds of vegetables and at differing stages of growth. There are lines of tall canes that come together at the top like narrow tents for the long green beans, higgledy-piggledy arrangements of large twigs with pea pods and leaves growing among them, long furrows of potato plants, some with white or purple flowers. After these, there's a massive cage with a door in it. Inside I can see small trees and bushes which I'm told provide fruit such as gooseberries, blackcurrants and raspberries. They are inside the cage to stop the birds getting to them. On the other side of a central path are rows of smaller plants: lettuce, radishes, spring onions. Each of these has an empty packet pegged into the ground to display a picture of the crop. Mum and Stella call these the salad vegetables. Also on this side is a shed with a climbing plant growing on a trellis like in the *Bill and Ben* TV programme. There are even flower pots of various sizes at the side and front. After the shed are rows of flowers, some the same as I've seen in vases in Aunt Stella's flat, and then a greenhouse with tomato plants. Each side of this section of the garden is bigger than the allotment I've seen my Grandad work on at the backs of Oxford Gardens.

At the far end of this section is a tall, prickly hedge. It's overgrown but there is a passage through to an area that has piles of grass cuttings, dead flowers, leaves and things. And then there is a darker place which is like a small forest with long grass in parts. It's the orchard and you can see tiny apples and pears appearing among the leaves. Through the trees I can just make out a low picket gate. Aunt Stella says it's kept locked to prevent people like me from wandering into the next part of the garden. Apparently, the land there slopes into a very marshy area so children aren't allowed.

I reckon I could easily climb over that gate. Maybe next time we visit, I can escape from the grown-ups for a while and explore. I'm wondering what section of the garden comes after the marshy part. In my mind, this garden goes on forever – each section leading to another, revealing something new and waiting to be discovered. It's magical.

Christmas Eve

It's Christmas Eve and I'm in bed in my bedroom which is the box-room upstairs at the back of the house.

I shout, "Mum, Mum, *mum!*"

From downstairs: "What is it?"

"I can't sleep."

"Try counting sheep."

Later: "Mum, Mum, *mum!*"

"Haven't you gone to sleep yet?" (Silly question.)

"No – but the sheep have."

Much later, I hear the jingling of distant bells. I lift up a corner of the curtain just in time to glimpse Father Christmas and his sleigh before they disappear into the night sky.

Puzzling Lyrics

Before the films start at the Saturday morning cinema showing for kids, we're encouraged to sing a song as the words appear on the screen. It's something about being 'good citizens' and 'champions of the free'. A free what? That's what I don't get. We're not told. My grandad would probably say that the song sounds like a typical American-style import, infused with right-wing ideology and improperly making a noun out of an adjective. And I wouldn't have the faintest idea of what he's talking about until I'm much older.

And talking of cinema, why should Roy Rogers' horse remain 'honest and faithful right up to the *inn*'? What happens then? Does Trigger's loyalty and integrity suddenly cease once Roy nips in for a swift half? Is he like a guide dog who trips up his owner after it's let off the leash at the end of a shift? It's not until much later that I discover that cowboys in the wild west don't pronounce the word *end* properly.

Similarly problematic is why the singer of the nursery rhyme repeatedly enters and exits an eagle during his perambulations along the City Road. And how is such a thing even possible? The conundrum is resolved at the age of thirteen when I learn from Anthony Newley that the Eagle is in fact a pub and that the frequent visits there are contributing to his money problems. To Newley, though, it's a less pertinent question than 'Why does the weasel go pop, go pop, pop goes the weasel?'

And what's a young kid to make of 'My body lies over the ocean', particularly when the severely dismembered vocalist pleads for someone to 'bring back my body to me'? Equally baffling anatomically is Anne Shelton singing 'Lay down your arms and surrender to mine.'

Finally, this one is often on the wireless and it's also played at Wolves matches. It's about some bod who spends his time wandering along mountain tracks singing about an appsack on his back. What is an *appsack* and why is there a song about it?

ITYP

There are only ten months between me and my younger cousin John. If we want to set off a fit of the giggles, we just say the letters *ITYP* to each other. This refers to an episode on a summer's day in Nan Leadbetter's back garden.

John and I are sitting on the lawn eating egg sandwiches. John takes a bite and, deciding he's not keen on egg, tosses the remainder over the nearby hedge. Almost immediately a head appears accompanied by a hand holding aloft the partly consumed sarnie. "Is this your piece?" we are asked in a stern voice. How were we to know that Mrs Nadin next door had been on her hands and knees tending her vegetable patch when the unexpected comestible came to ground directly in front of her?

Our New Home

We're no longer living with my Nan at her house because we've moved into our own place at the other end of town. It's a new bungalow with a kitchen, living room, two bedrooms and a bathroom. Apparently, Mum and Dad have been able to buy a plot of land at a cheap price from the local council because they had something called 'established housing need'. There are lots of other houses in different stages of construction in our road, and there is a new estate being built almost opposite, but our family is one of the first to move in.

My parents call our plot 'the wilderness' because it is full of large weeds, long grass and bramble bushes. Dad says that after saving up all summer for a wheelbarrow, he can now make a start on taming it. And so each weekend, things appear in the garden. First to arrive are some large concrete blocks which Dad uses to build a front wall. Concrete fence posts come in ones and twos, sometimes with the odd roll of chain-link fencing, but always on a Saturday afternoon or a Sunday. Likewise the cement mixer which disappears during the week, although the bags of cement remain. A front lawn is beginning to develop and this gets a little larger each time we visit Cannock Chase. There is a spade permanently in the boot of Dad's car. He tells me it's OK if you cut out just a few turves, and from a different place each time, as it soon grows back.

Mum's face has an anxious look whenever she enquires about the source of all these things, but Dad tells her not to worry. But she does. She's so honest she's been known to go past her stop if the bus conductor has not yet collected her fare. Today, though, Mum's anxiety has turned to anger and it looks as though Dad will be in for it when he gets back this evening. It's Monday morning and a workman from the building site across the road has just called. He's asking if we've seen any half-inch gravel as their pile is somewhat depleted. He doesn't seem too convinced by Mum's answer as he crunches his way back down our new driveway.

The Ration Book and the Divi Number

We've not long moved to our new house. There are lots of houses and other buildings still being built and there are neat stacks of bricks and window frames, cement mixers and shovels, boxes of nails and scaffolding joints dotted over quite a wide area. In fact, everything that kids of our age could wish for when playing Cowpokes and Indians or, more likely, re-enacting key battles from the war. (Even though the Second World War ended a couple of years before most of us were born, adults still talk about it as though it were just yesterday and apparently there are lots of films and books about it.)

There is no playing soldiers for me this morning, though. I've been sent with shopping list and ration book to the Co-op over the road. It's housed temporarily in a long prefabricated building because the permanent store has only just begun to be built. There are long lines of customers each leading to a different shop assistant standing behind the counter which runs the entire length of the building. I join the back of one of the queues. There are long periods of time when none of the queues seems to be moving at all. Then someone will leave and one of the lines will shuffle up a couple of feet. But mine doesn't budge. I should have chosen a different one. Shall I do that now… oh, it is moving a bit now. This process is repeated endlessly, or so it feels. I eventually reach the high counter. The problem is it's so high that five-year-olds can't see over it – and shopworkers can't see me. I lose count of the adults who don't see me, or pretend not to, and are served first.

Someone at last takes pity on me and draws the attention of the assistant who leans over to take the shopping list from my up-stretched hand. Each item is placed into a brown paper bag which she closes by deftly using both hands to spin it over a couple times. I hand her up some money and the ration book. I say, "Forty-two," when I'm asked for my Co-op Divi Number and wait for the inevitable "Not your house number, love, your Divi number." I may only be five but I'm already tired of this response and insist that forty-two is indeed our Divi Number. I don't add the explanation that ours is a lot smaller than the usual five-figure number owing to its original issue to my mother's father who used to manage a Co-op store in town. Although the Stafford Co-operative Society had been founded in 1860, it merged with a neighbouring town in 1939 to become the Stafford & Stone Co-op. Grandfather and his family were among the first to be given the new membership cards.

I return home with the shopping only to undergo a parental interrogation as to why the simple errand has taken me all of two hours. It's no wonder that children want to be older than we are – we can't wait to be taller.

A Mundane Misery

What is worse than the routine misery of being dragged round town by your mum on a cold, wet day – in and out of shops, waiting in queues, around the draughty market stalls, especially the smelly ones that stink of rotting vegetables?

One thing that's worse is the bus journey home. It's always crowded. A kid my size gets squashed between his mum and the next adult stranger in the compressed line of passengers standing between the rows of seats and hanging onto the leather straps that dangle from the ceiling. I'm not tall enough to reach so you grab whatever you can to keep your balance as the bus sways and bumps its way along the Wolverhampton Road. And the nearer you are towards the open back of the vehicle the colder it is with the icy wind whipping the back of your legs as you long for the day when you're old enough for long trousers. Every time the bus stops people push past you to reach the exit, not noticing small children beneath them as they tread on your toes and drag their wet coats or shopping bags across your face. And if it's not a passenger, it's the bad-tempered bus conductor in the fingerless gloves banging her ticket machine into the back of your head as she grumbles up and down the packed gangway. If you do manage to get a seat, you have to give it up again when a grown-up gets on. And all the time there's a choking aroma of tobacco smoke and stale sweat. I'm not surprised that all Midland Red buses have notices saying *NO HAWKING OR SPITTING*. But this doesn't stop the cacophony of wheezing, spluttering, chest-rattling coughing and determined nose-blowing that doesn't let up for the entire journey.

So there's nothing worse than catching the bus home on a cold, wet, windy day. Except for not catching the bus home on a cold, wet, windy day. This happened recently when for some reason there were no buses. We had to walk all the way home in the cold and rain and wind. With all the shopping. That is even worse.

Been There, Done That

I've been looking forward to this day for a long time. I've been prepared for it and the grey blazer with the green piping and the badge on the pocket has been bought. It's the day I go to school – Rising Brook County Primary School, Infants Department.

Mum takes me to the green school gates, but there's really no need. It's not far away and I know how to get there. There are loads of other kids at the gates. Some are weeping and wailing, hanging on tightly to their mothers. Cry-babies. I can't wait to get inside and I tell mum she can go now.

Through the high doors and it's all much bigger than I thought. There are buildings on all sides of a patch of green grass which would be good to play football on but a man in blue overalls is doing something to it with a fork. Some of the buildings are tall and there are lots of windows. There is a corridor which runs along all the edges of the lawn. Everywhere there's a peculiar smell I've not come across before – it's neither pleasant nor unpleasant, just a bit mysterious.

I'm taken to my classroom which is on the ground floor and at a far corner. It's very big and has a sand pit at one end. I meet my teacher who wears a sort of pinafore and is called Mrs Chiltern. She introduces me to someone called Graham Mead whose feet turn in when he walks.

It's quite warm when we leave at the end of the day and I carry my blazer over my shoulder by putting a finger through the hanging loop as I've seen the older boys do. Mum is at the gates to collect me, eager to find how my day has been. I tell her all about it as we walk home together.

The next day I am the one in tears at the school gate. Mum can't understand why I'm kicking up so much fuss as, with the help of at least two teachers, she tries to dislodge me from the green railings to which I'm desperately clinging. In all the no-doubt well-meaning preparations which my parents had put in place, it would have been helpful to point out that attendance at school is meant to be more than a one-off experience.

Coronation and Lipstick

It's the day of Queen Elizabeth II's coronation. We go round to Uncle Frank and Auntie Nora's house to watch it on their television. It is boring. Lots of pictures of moving carriage wheels and soldiers in old-fashioned uniforms and silly hats.

On another day, Mum takes me to this sort of party in a big wooden hut just up the road from where we are now living. It's like a party because there are quite a few kids there and there's sandwiches, jelly, pink blancmange and orange juice. But there are too many adults there – all mums I think – for it to be a proper party. They are doing things that grown-ups don't usually do, such as dancing something called the hokey-cokey. They are in a circle and kicking their legs into the air which makes the floorboards bounce and clatter.

It's all rather unseemly, particularly as some of these women are wearing green tweedy-type suits and lipstick – that awful bright-red lipstick. A long time ago, when I was about two or three, I was waiting with my mum at the Pitcher Bank bus stop in town. There was a woman in a green coat lying on the pavement making loud wailing noises and I saw blood all round her mouth. A couple of people in the queue helped her up and slowly half-walked half-carried her, still weeping, into the pet shop behind the bus stand. It was much later before I realised that it was probably thickly and unskilfully applied lipstick which I'd witnessed, rather than blood. And it has put me off lipstick. My mum wears it occasionally, although it's not one of the deep red varieties. Even so, I dislike the smell of it when she spits on her hanky to wipe dirt off my face.

After a game of pass the parcel, when very many layers of newspaper are peeled off and someone wins something, we are each given a silver-coloured spoon and something my mother calls a serviette ring to take home. On each is some sort of emblem to do with the coronation. A few of the children are also presented with mugs with a picture of the queen and the duke of Edinburgh on. I think they are for those kids who hadn't already received one from school. We keep our toothbrushes in mine.

We leave the green hut just as it's beginning to get dark. You can still make out the red, white and blue on the little flags around the doorway and at the bottom of the roof. They remind me of my favourite pair of ankle socks.

The Woman Who Cleans Up the Sick

"Who is that lady?" asks my mother after I've been brought home from school early, with a bandaged finger, by Miss Bowkley. I reply, "She's the woman who cleans the sick up."[1]

To my knowledge there has been no sick to be dealt with today, but other tasks await. That afternoon, I'm fully occupied in gun-making in Miss Biggin's class. Pupils have been told to select pieces of wood and any other materials from the large crate at the front of the classroom – and to 'make something' from them. Just as Michaelangelo could envisage his statue in a block of marble, I can see the handgun in the few pieces of scrap wood I've selected.

As I'm nearly six and in my second year of Infants School, I'm allowed to use a hammer and a few small nails (yes, really!). I soon become engrossed in the task and it seems no time at all before Miss Biggin instructs us all to return the tools and make our way back to our tables. I'm sitting on the floor and panicking now because I haven't quite finished. Panic turns to tears of frustration as I'm almost the only one still on the floor. Desperate to complete my gun, my hammering speeds to a reckless frenzy. I sense that

---

1   Trainee teachers are often given the worst jobs to do.

everyone must now be in their seats and looking down on me. Suddenly I hear a girl say, "Please Miss, David Roberts is crying because he's bleeding everywhere!"

Sure enough, I look down and for the first time I notice blood, and there's quite a lot of it. It's on my would-be gun, my clothes, the floor… but most of it is on and around my thumb from which it continues to flow. It's also only then I feel physical pain. My thumb hurts – although I'm still far more concerned about my incomplete project. And now it's a bit sticky and red in places.

From down the corridor Miss Bowkley is summoned. I'm taken to the room with the first-aid box and bandaged up. As the bandage soon starts to turn red, it's decided that I'll be taken home. Miss Bowkley no doubt has my address but seems unsure how to get there even though it's not far. I take her a long way round – partly as I'm uncertain that Mum will yet be back from work, but mainly because I want to show the Sick Lady I'm quite capable of negotiating a complicated route home by myself.

We arrive at my house and mother is in. She seems alarmed by the large red bandage. Miss Bowkley seeks to reassure her before hurrying off back to school; there may yet still be some sick to clean up before the school-day ends.

Knee-socks and Scabs

Winter is approaching so it's time for one of those boyhood rites of passage: my very first pair of knee-socks. They are grey, of course, with two green hoops in the folded-back section just below the knee. The green is slightly lighter, and brighter, than that of the piped edging of my blazer, but it still looks great.

Dad must have finished work early because I see our Morris Minor as I come out of school. I run towards it.

Sneaking a few glances at my socks to see how they look when moving quickly, I don't see the lump in the pavement until I meet it at full tilt. I know, as I'm in slow-motion flight, that the landing will be painful. In tears, I pick up the now somewhat battered shoe-box house with cellophane windows that I've made in school and hobble to the car. Straightening my legs, I examine the blood from my knees trickle onto my new socks – perilously close to the green hoops. I immediately cheer up when Dad tells me not to worry it'll soon scab up.

He's right. It's not long before I'm proudly parading the playground with a couple of impressive crusties. My uniform is complete: blazer, hoop-topped knee-socks, double scabs. I'm a proper schoolboy now.

The Smell of Tarmac in the Morning

I love the smell of new-mown grass and freshly laid tarmac.

We're treated to a really good dose of the latter as we reach the final stages of our route march from the old school at Rising Brook to our brand new one which is called Highfields. We are walking, class-by-class with our teachers between the two, a distance of half a mile. It's only we Infants pupils who are moving today, the Juniors' playground is still being spread with the sweet-smelling black stuff. Ours has already been done and topped with the finely ground pebbly stuff so we can get gravel-rash when we fall over.

The new school is terrific. At the front and back of the massive hall the windows go from the floor to the ceiling. All the toilets and washbasins are inside. Our classroom is right at the end so you can see the lawns and playing fields on three sides. Through the open windows we can smell the grass being cut by a large green tractor.

I think I'm going to like this school.

Trolleybuses

I enjoy going on the train to Wolverhampton with Mum on one of her occasional shopping trips there. An enormous department store called Beatties has so many floors – and each floor has hundreds of sections – that it is easy to get lost. And a lot of kids get separated from their mums because messages are always coming over the Tannoy about children being ready for collection from the tea counter in the cafe. And this is where we sometimes meet up with Auntie Sheila and drink tea out of green cups. I used to think that Sheila's sister owns the entire place because she has the same name as the store. Sheila travels in from Bloxwich by trolleybus. I'm fascinated by the trolleybuses – and all their associated overhead wiring – and they're the main reason I like going to Wolverhampton. We don't have them in our town.

Choosing my Little Brother's Name

We'll write all the possibles on small tabs of paper and you can draw just one out of the hat. This is what we'll call your new baby brother. These are the instructions my parents have given me. Quite a responsibility for someone yet to reach his seventh birthday. It is many years later before I twig that all the tabs would have had 'Michael' on them.[2]

Rich

It's my seventh birthday and I'm opening my presents in my parents' bedroom. I think this is because on this cold

---

2   I don't think I felt cheated. By then I probably realised that it was an attempt to give me an ownership stake in the family's new arrival. It worked.

April morning it is the warmest room in the house, with the paraffin stove having been lit specially.

There are no super-large or strange shaped packages this year. Most of the gifts come in envelopes together with the greetings cards (not very interesting) because I'm receiving mainly money (more interesting). This has probably got something to do with the new baby who arrived a few weeks ago. Apparently my family, including the grans, have been a bit preoccupied with matters other than the question of what to get for my birthday.

But that's OK with me. It's now a bit later and I'm alone in the room. For what could well be the tenth time I'm counting the money. On the large bed, I'm placing the coins into wobbly silver piles according to denomination: half-crowns, florins, shilling pieces and sixpences. I have forty-two shillings and I'm rich.

Hola Amigos

I don't know if it's my persistence or if they are bored with the film, but somehow I manage to persuade my parents that we leave the matinee at the *Odeon* early. I'm desperate to get home to watch *The Cisco Kid* on TV. It will be the very first programme I'll see on our own television. The set arrived this morning; we've never had one before.

Cisco himself is a bit too flashy: his clothes make him look like that comedian called Max Miller. I prefer Cisco's partner, Pancho. At the end of each episode, Cisco says 'Adios amigos' and Pancho adds a 'See you soon, aha!' before they ride off into the rocky distance.

Cowboy sidekicks seem to be a requirement of TV westerns. While Cisco has his Pancho, the masked and loosely corseted Lone Ranger has his Tonto and the multi-tasselled Range Rider his Dick.

And God Said…

We're big boys and girls now. We've moved up from the Infants to the Junior School where everything is larger – the school hall, the tables and chairs, the toilets, even the teachers are taller, I think.

Miss Stirland is reading us a bible story. Something from the Old Testament, she says. You can tell from her voice and because she's stretching to a standing position that she's coming to an important bit:

"And God Said… Barry Morton *sit down!*"

You can't ignore an instruction like that, so Barry freezes, mid-wander, and then obeys.

It hasn't been Barry's week. A couple of days ago, we were about to start the end-of-the-day quick prayer ritual.

"Right, children: chairs on desks, hands together, eyes shut."

The teacher's first line of prayer is interrupted with a "Please Miss, David Roberts has got his eyes open."

Some of the kids in the class don't immediately get why it is Barry, not I, who goes on to suffer the sharp edge of Miss Stirland's tongue. But I think Barry had twigged even before Miss had finished her pre-reproval glare.

Monday, Monday

James T always wears his mac for school on Mondays and he doesn't take it off all day. He won't tell us why – but the teacher lets him keep it on. By crawling under the table one of the other kids discovers that James is not wearing trousers.

James eventually discloses that this is the day they are washed.

All the clothes lines in the area are fully occupied every Monday, but rarely on other days. I think there must be a law that states you must wash clothes on a Monday and only on a Monday. It doesn't explain why James always wears wellies, though.

A Joyous Lesson

Mr Edwards – pale-blue shirt-sleeves rolled up, tie tucked between shirt buttons – is demonstrating volume equivalence and ratio with the aid of a full tin bath and vessels of various capacities. His enthusiastic scooping and transfer from one to another is sending waves of water over the floor, and Mr E's clothing is turning the soggy side of damp. There can't be anyone in the rapt audience of fifty or so eight-year-olds who will now ever forget that two pints make a quart or that four quarts equal a gallon.

A disapproving face peers through the glass in the door. Legs apart, raised pint glass in one hand, dripping saucepan in the other, our instructor turns his head as the door opens a few inches. "Are you *teaching*, Mr Edwards?" enquires the doubting face. Mr E is beckoned outside for a hushed consultation. A brilliant lesson is being frowned upon by a killjoy of a Head Teacher.

First Loves

Caroline
She is in my class and I love everything about her. I don't think I'd like to meet her parents, though – her father is the Headmaster of the big school that the older kids go to so he must be rather frightening. I don't imagine that will happen in any case since Caroline doesn't know what I think of her.

Helen

In our second year of junior school, we sit in pairs in rows according to our positions in class at the end of the previous school year. Helen sits in front of me because she came second. She sits next to Alan Moss who came first. I wish I'd come top so I could sit next to her. It would be easier to ask her out. So I write her a letter instead, inviting her to the pictures to see a film. I also promise in the letter to buy her a box of Cadbury Roses chocolates. I put a stamp on the envelope and post the letter in the pillar box.

Now I'm panicking. I'm not sure I've done the right thing. What if her parents read the letter or worse, what if Helen doesn't want to go on a date and jokes about it with her friends? My parents can see I'm bothered about something and eventually I confess. They tell me not to worry. They'll go to her house this evening and explain things to Helen's mum and dad before the letter arrives tomorrow. That sounds like a good plan.

I'm not sure what's been concerning me the most. Is it the embarrassment I'd feel at being laughed about or the hurt of a rejection? Or is it that on my pocket money I can barely afford one cinema ticket, never mind two *and* a box of Roses? Whatever the reason, my love for Helen is not diminished and I'm bereft when, not much later, she and her family move to Worthing.

Andrea

A new girl has joined our class and I'm immediately attracted to her. I like her face and her pony tail. She tells me where she lives and says it's OK to call round for her on Saturday. I look forward to it all week as, in my mind, I'm already starting to see Andrea as my girlfriend.

There's a long garden leading to her front door but I see her straight away. She's sitting on the large front lawn.

She suggests a country walk but we first have to wait for her friend. I hadn't banked on this, but I suppose a walk with two girls might still be OK and wonder to myself what the other girl will be like. The new friend soon arrives and Andrea does the introductions. "This is Martin – my boyfriend."

Jane

The Head Teacher says the three of us – with our guitar, home-made bass and washboard – can perform *Tom Dooley* at the school concert, provided we are singing along to the record. The volume of the small Dansette record player in the large school hall isn't great and is soon drowned out by the enthusiasm of our performance. It seems to go down well despite the fact that our version of the song ends a few bars ahead of Lonnie Donegan's.

While we are singing, I notice that Jane from 4B is staring at me – or at least in my general direction. After the concert, feeling something of a celebrity and with my guitar slung over my shoulder, I'm about to head home through the school gates when there's a knock on the corner classroom window. It's Jane. She opens the window slightly and starts asking me about my skiffle group. We seem to be getting on well so I ask if she'd like to go for a walk and I'll show her my guitar. Before she can answer, the stern expression of Mr Harford appears behind her. It says, "Hop it, son."

The Best Christmas Present

Christmas Day and the best Christmas present is my first full Wolves kit: old-gold shirt with the black cuffs and collar, black shorts and hooped black and gold socks. There's also a pair of genuine black leather Bert Williams football boots with his signature in white-lettering. I already know about

the boots, though, as my grandad took me to Bert's own sports shop in Bilston a few weeks ago to try them on. I also know they cost a lot of money – about three pounds ten shillings I think. And it was the great man himself who helped me into the boots and lace them up properly. While we were there, we also bought a tin of dubbin – lovely stuff.

Before lunch we meet up with Brian and John at the house of Uncle Frank's friend, Bill Giles, and we play football with his son in their large back garden. I'm wearing my new kit. The shorts are rather big – the waistband almost reaches my chest. Apparently, I'll grow into them.

A Dislike of Hats

I think there's a law that once a man reaches the age of twenty-one he should wear a hat. Most of the men I know don either a flat cap or a trilby when they go out. You can barely see Mr Dulcamara, the tiny insurance man with the bicycle clips, under his a gigantic grey trilby with a silk band. Mum says that, strictly speaking, his is not a trilby but a fedora.

I see another one a bit like it when Dad takes me to see Stafford Rangers play. One of the linesmen hasn't turned up and his place is taken by a man in ordinary clothes. The wind keeps blowing his hat off as he's running up and down the line with his flag. The crowd on our side are laughing at him until he turns round and starts to swear at us. The crowd, including Dad, is shouting and swearing back (a lot of the words begin with 'b'), telling him to keep his eye on the game.

Most of the men in the crowd have caps on. It is raining, though, so I suppose they do serve some purpose. Even Dad is wearing one today even though he doesn't normally put anything on his head. I notice, though, that for the past few weeks there's also been a trilby on the parcel shelf of our car. Dad says it's because he's been told off by his boss for not wearing a hat – and for sporting suede shoes – when making calls as a sales rep. It's just for emergencies, he says; he doesn't put it on unless the boss is around. And he still wears the suedes.

Mum seems to share this aversion to hats. On the few occasions she feels forced to wear one, she grumbles as she sticks pins the size of knitting needles through the sides of her hat and into her hair. It looks rather dangerous to me: you could do a lot of damage with skewers of that enormity. I think Mum's dislike of hats is why she doesn't often go to church.

Advantages and Disadvantages of Little Brothers

It's a Saturday and through the open window of the car I can already hear the calls of the seagulls. A little later as we drive over the brow of the hill, I can see the sea below us. For those of us who live in the middle of the country and are lucky to experience the view just once a year at best, it's a truly wondrous sight.

We're about to start our week's holiday at the seaside. But by Tuesday it's all over and I'm informed of our impending premature return home. I'm allowed a final drizzly half-hour with my bucket and spade on the beach before we load up the car and I'm waving a teary goodbye through the rear window to the rapidly disappearing sea front.

I'm on the rear seat next to my little brother's carry-cot. And it's my little brother who is the cause of my sadness and the reason for the early end to our holiday. Apparently, Michael has barely slept since our arrival at the house where we are staying. Mum and Dad say he just won't settle and cries all night keeping them – and no doubt the owners of the house in the next room – awake. It's news to me. I'm in the little third bedroom and have not heard a thing. I've been sleeping fine.

I look down at little brother as the car continues to climb the hill out of town. He's fast asleep. As Dad drives, he and Mum are leaning towards each other in whispered conversation. Mum turns to address me. In compensation for missing out on half my holiday ("More than half," I correct her), how would I like a bicycle, a brand new one?

What a silly question to ask an eight-year-old. But I'm not thinking this as in an instant my despair turns to joy. And sure enough, a few days later I take charge of a beautiful bright-red Raleigh bike. My first two-wheeler. It has an eighteen-inch frame and twenty-four-inch wheels.

A bike lasts longer than a holiday – and I did have (almost) half a holiday as well. So there are upsides as well as disadvantages to having a little brother.

World War III?

I thought it was something to do with blocked drains but apparently it's about a canal in Egypt, and it's spelt S-u-e-z. I don't know the details but Dad has a lot of things called petrol coupons in his wallet. And whatever it is that's happening in the canal, it's the reason why there's a collection of large drums of fuel in the garage. Dad says he needs them for work but I'm not to tell anyone about them. Also, Richard Loveridge is running around the playground being a Russian warplane because there's going to be another world war. I don't like the sound of that.

Roping in the Local Kids

There's a long, thick rope being carried along the street by a man and a line of children. We're curious, of course – we're children.

"Where are you going with that rope, mister?"

"Join on the end and see."

So we do – we are children. And none of us has yet heard the word paedophile – although I think we all know of some men who are a bit strange. But we continue to tour the local streets and to collect more kids for our rope line. This is exciting. Soon, even though we're all bunched up close, there is no spare rope left. The man at the front leads us into a tall, unfriendly looking building. It's a bit scary but there are a lot of us and we have a rope to hold onto.

Not for much longer, though. The man seems to lose interest in the rope and tells us to leave it on the floor as he ushers us through another set of doors into a vast cavern with long light-brown wooden seats. We're invited to sit on the first few rows. The man then talks to us in a loud voice about Jesus and Sunday Schools. This goes on for a very long time. Judging by the anxious looks on the faces of those children I can see when I look around, I don't think I'm the only one who wants to leave. But nobody makes a move of that sort.

I don't recall how it all ends. Thinking back to the start of the adventure, I did wonder about the funny collar and black buttonless shirt beneath the man's jacket. I find out later that the big building is the recently built Nonconformist church that has just opened. I decide I'm not a fan of the recruitment tactics of Methodism.

Silly Sod

Little brother has learned how to climb out of his cot. He then nosedives onto my bed. And he's doing it repeatedly. Each time I have to get up and put him back into his cage. It's annoying so I move his cot away from my bed. There's a noise – something between a thud and a crack – then a few seconds silence before alternating loud screams and sobbing intakes of breath bring my parents running into the room. Guess who gets the blame for the silly sod landing head-first on the hard tiled floor.

Watch With Brother

Often during the school holidays I have to stay with little brother while he watches the early afternoon television programme for little kids. The series is called *Watch With Mother* but ours is usually busy doing something else.

On Mondays, it's *Picture Book*. The content is varied but normally boring. Tuesdays is the oh-so-nice *Andy Pandy*. He's what people of my parents' generation call a 'big girl's blouse', whatever that is. I just think he's a sissy in a fussy romper suit. The best of the week by far appears each Wednesday. Bill and Ben are the *Flower Pot Men*. They speak a strange language but you can tell what they are saying by how their voices go up and down. The stories are good because each week they get into some trouble from which they are usually saved by their stationary friend Little Weed before the gardener returns to his shed.

Thursdays are a low point. *Rag, Tag and Bobtail*, a trio of puppets supposedly representing country animals (hedgehog, mouse, rabbit), is painfully slow. Three snails would be more appropriate. The first part of each episode consists of the three wee creatures greeting each other –

one at a time and with every single word stretched to its pronounceable limits.

"Hello Rag."

"Hello Tag."

Bobtail crawls onto the scene at a very un-rabbit-like pace.

"Hello Rag."

"Hello Bobtail."

"Hello Tag."

"Hello Bobtail."

This is frustratingly tedious. The introductions take so long there's barely time for any story to develop before the pals are bidding their mutual farewells, once again taking an inordinate length of time to do so.

"Goodbye Rag."

"Goodbye Tag."

"Goodbye Rag."

"Goodbye Bobtail."

"Goodbye..." and so on, and on.

By this time my brother and I have switched off, mentally if not always literally.

Things are on the up again on Fridays, though. *The Woodentops* is the most recent addition to the series and I was unsure about it at first. It's about this rather stupid family who live in the country. It grows on you after a while, perhaps because of the escapades of the family pet, 'the very biggest spotty dog you ever did see'. It's still a few rungs below *Bill & Ben*, though.

Honesty Pays

I find two shillings and ninepence (a half-crown and three pennies) behind the green junction box towards the bottom of Burton Manor Road. In the red phone box opposite, the

Post Office is experimenting with an emergency button as a quicker way of being put through to the police, fire or ambulance services. Instead of using this to say rude words to the operator, as some of us have been rumoured to do on the way home from school, I ask to be put through to the police to report my find. They must be taking it seriously as I'm instructed to take the coins to the main police station in town – immediately.

Dad, though, downplays its importance, but not wishing to deter my honesty promises to take me there later. After duly reporting the details, and watching the policeman laboriously writing them down in a large book, I'm invited to take the money away with me. I'm told that if it remains unclaimed after three months I can keep it.

I last out for nearly four weeks, which I think is pretty good going.

Politics and Chocolate

Each Saturday morning my dad visits his father's house for an argument about politics, and he takes me with him. While Grandad and Dad – and often my Uncle Geoff, too – get into long and sometimes heated discussions about Nye Bevan or Anthony Eden or Suez or the NHS, I sit in the old and saggy chair with the wooden arms in front of a blazing coal fire. We are all in the tiny back room with the small cast-iron range to the side and the old flat iron propping open the door to the back kitchen whence flows the ever-present smell of sheep or pig lights which grandmother boils up for the equally smelly cat. It's cosy, though, and warm.

For me, the highlight of the morning is when Grandad takes me through to the high, dimly lit, floor-tiled hallway at the front part of the house. Bending slightly, he slowly lifts the lid of the massive wooden chest but only by just enough to, even more slowly, slip his other hand inside. As a weak beam of light from the fanlight above the front door momentarily puts a shine on Grandad's bald head, he ever-so-gradually pulls out a bar of Cadbury's milk chocolate before allowing the heavy lid to slam shut until next week. As he ceremoniously hands me the bar I check to see if this week it contains fruit and nuts (not so good), nuts only (better) or whether it's plain chocolate (the best). All this takes place in silence but I just know that the chest must be crammed full from top to bottom with slabs of chocolate because Grandad never has to reach far inside to retrieve one. There must be hundreds and hundreds.

Rude Words

Elder cousin Brian is at the big school. Among his school books, John – his younger brother – and I come across an English-French dictionary. We decide to add a few entries of our own. On the inside of the hardback cover, we write all the swear words we can think of – there's quite a lot. We're thinking it's a good joke: Brian will open his book in class, see the list of profanities and have to close it again quickly. At worst, he may get into a bit of trouble if the teacher sees it.

Trouble follows very quickly, but it's not Brian who is in it – at least not yet. He discovers our attempts to boost his lexical range and John and I are each confronted by angry parents. Apparently, the dictionary is not school issue but has been loaned to Brian personally by his French teacher. So, it's rather embarrassing all round. And not just that: it looks like John and I will be forfeiting a few weeks' pocket money to pay for a replacement.

Our Nan tells us it's OK to say those words, but not a good idea to write them down. I think we've found that out for ourselves, Nan.

Highwaymen Should Speak More Clearly

I don't understand that peculiar instruction issued by highwaymen. 'Stand on your liver', they demand as they point their pistols at the unfortunate occupants of the stagecoach. To me this seems an extremely messy, if not impossible, thing to ask of someone, and totally unnecessary for relieving them of their personal possessions.

When eventually the correct saying is explained to me, I blame it on the poor diction of Dick Turpin and his mates, rather than my ears. It's another fault to add to their list of dastardly deeds. I wonder why their acts of daylight robbery are presented so romantically. Although they're sometimes portrayed as Robin Hood characters, I don't hear much about any great wealth distribution having taken place. Perhaps it's the masks. That and the peculiar hats that don't seem to fall off as they gallop off with the loot.

I've heard that Dick Turpin is supposed to have stayed overnight at the Goat's Head in Abbots Bromley after stealing Black Bess from the Rugeley Horse Fair on his ride to York. It's probably all part of the made-up stories that have grown out of the Turpin legend. I'd like it to be true because an ancestor of mine was the inn's landlord at one stage, and there are other long-dead relatives buried in the nearby churchyard.

A Plague of Boils

All of us, except Dad, have had boils for a while so Mum is insisting we all take these big, unpleasant yeast tablets and have hot baths. Our hot tank can't cope with all of this extra demand and the water soon runs cold. Mum then brings in supplements which have been boiling away in kettle and large saucepans in the kitchen. Pouring these into the bath so close to my legs seems a bit risky to me but Mum tells me not to fuss. After soaking our boils for a while, something called Basilicon ointment, which is a nice yellow colour, is applied. Apparently it's supposed to draw the pustule to a head so that it bursts more quickly and all this yucky stuff comes out.

The treatment seems to be working as mine are almost cleared up now – except for a very large, crimson eruption just below the belly button. It's really quite sore and Mum says it's more like an abscess. Having the hot bath seems to help but I won't need the ointment today. I take extra care with the towel but forget about it when putting on my new underpants. The elastic in the waistband is powerful and snaps right against the tender protrusion. There's more blood than pus but it's the yell that causes mother's rapid reappearance in the bathroom.

Den Envy

Kids like building dens. You can build a den from almost anything. One of our first after moving to this end of town is in one of those gigantic concrete cylindrical things that are used for laying drains or sewers or something. You just block off one end with bricks or pieces of wood or whatever's around and you have a den. It's surprising the number of kids you can get inside. It can get a bit uncomfortable if you spend too long in there. We discover that when this older boy warns us about a dangerous wild cat in the vicinity which can bite right through human bones. He says our safest bet is to stay where we are while he arranges for some adults to rescue us. We must have been there for hours but no-one comes to help. Eventually the boy nearest the open end bravely ventures outside. He says the coast is clear, and we all go home. We never see a wild cat.

As we get older, our dens get more ambitious. Lots of new houses are still being built near us so there are piles of bricks and other building stuff all over the place. After the workmen have knocked off we can spend the evenings, Saturday afternoons and Sundays on our own constructions. We soon learn that walls made of a double-layer of cross-laid and interwoven house bricks can be quite sturdy without the need for mortar. At any rate, they easily support a roof of corrugated iron sheeting. As we get more adventurous, our dens begin to resemble smallish dwellings as we experiment with gaps for windows as well as doorways and with constructing internal walls to form more than one room. But when we try to put together some sort of fireplace complete with some piping for a chimney, we have to evacuate the place in a hurry when the smoke fails to go where it's supposed to.

Remarkably, sometimes our work remains intact for a few weeks. The builders on the site seem to leave them alone until they need the bricks for the more permanent houses they are constructing. Our dens are more at risk from marauders from the estate on the other side of the main road. Every so often they take delight in kicking down our walls or throwing bricks onto the roof. And one time they demolish our den while we are in it. We form a retaliatory gang to enter their territory but we don't find any dens. I think all the houses over there have already been built so they don't have the materials. They probably attack ours out of envy.

Lessons from a Greenfinch

It's a late Spring morning on what is promising to be a very warm day and we're walking the public footpath to our primary school. A sound or sight from the hedgerow attracts someone's attention and we find a greenfinch in some distress. It seems to be caught in something, repeated attempts to get away are making things worse and the bird is soon hanging limply. It looks like its head is snared in some sort of thread or wire which has been tied to a branch of the hedge.

We're not able to free the head but eventually one of us manages to break the thread next to the branch and the finch, still limp but still alive, is carried carefully into school. The headteacher is at the far end of the hall in front of the vast bank of windows, preparing for that morning's assembly. We know he has an interest in the natural world for it's often the subject of his school talks. Gently, he takes charge of the bird and with skill and tenderness somehow manages to free the creature from its noose. All the time, the Head talks quietly to us, explaining that the bird is quite young and that it's a victim of a deliberate attempt to trap birds. The bird continues to lie still in his rescuer's now open hand for a few seconds before suddenly flying off at speed – but straight into one of the large window panes. We dash to where it has fallen but it is dead, its neck broken.

After assembly, the Head asks to be shown the place in the hedgerow where the finch was found so he could check for any other traps that might be there. I'm certain that his main motive is to prevent further suffering but I also suspect he feels some guilt at being in part responsible for ending, as well as saving, a life. So perhaps today is helping me to learn that human beings have a great capacity for compassion but they can also, like the trapper, commit acts of premeditated cruelty. And that even adult heroes aren't perfect.

Uncomfortable Socks

Mum always buys me socks that are at least a size too big. It's so 'I can grow into them'. The problem is that in the meantime the ends have to be tucked under my toes before I put on my shoes. And this is uncomfortable. And the socks are woollen which makes it even worse. Especially when they get wet – which happens when you walk into snowdrifts and the snow goes over the top of your wellies. Which means for the rest of the day, until you get home for tea, you're feet are not just wet but cold, too.

And by the time you've grown into them the socks have been darned so many times that the discomfort persists. It never goes away. I hate woollen socks.

Coming to think of it, though, I don't like any clothes made of wool: high-necked jumpers, gloves, pullover sleeves that are longer than those of my shirt. They all 'fridge' me – which is a word Mum uses to describe the very unpleasant feeling that I get with wool directly next to my skin. The word has nothing to do with the abbreviation for refrigerator. We don't have one of those and we don't know anyone who has so that use of the word is not part of our daily discourse.

But by far the worst are knitted balaclavas. My whole face crawls and bits of wool get in your mouth. Balaclavas are a totally unnecessary item of childhood clothing. Kids don't feel cold on their faces.

Bostin Fittle

Sausage and mash. Serve with a lot of butter. Adding a fried egg is optional.

Dripping on toast. Spread the dripping straight from the greaseproof paper packet onto hot toast. The packet with red lettering contains beef dripping; mutton dripping has blue – or is it the other way round? Mum just sends me to Boydens' Butchers for a packet of each. The shop is owned by two brothers. One of them wears a navy blue apron with thin white stripes. The other, fatter, brother is usually in a light-brown coat-type overall with sleeves and buttons, although I've also seen him in a red and white striped apron. His face has the look and colour of one of the pig's heads on display, but Mum tells me that's cruel.

Apple & sugar sandwiches. The apple should be sliced, never grated.

Suet pudding. I don't like too much treacle on it, though. Very nice with thick custard.

Raw peas. Freshly picked from Dad's vegetable garden and eaten direct from the shell whilst seated outside on a kitchen chair. Mum gives me a colander and indicates the amount needed for dinner. I need to pick three times this quantity as they're very moreish.

Proper hot dogs. None of your limp, plastic-coated frankfurters and pappy baps. These are real pork sausages placed inside crunchy bridge rolls with a thick layer of butter which drips down your chin when you bite into them.

Fruit sponge without the fruit. With thick custard. If the sponge is not quite cooked through at the centre, all the better.

Chips. The ones I have at home are probably the best, but a six of chips from old Mrs Snape's in Sandon Road is normally pretty good, too. Best to avoid if there's much of a queue, though: it can take her quite a while to fold the sheets of newspaper and put each portion into them. Once a week we have fish (usually haddock which I prefer to cod) with the chips. This is always on a Friday. I gather we never have meat on that day for reasons of religious tradition. I don't understand this, my only friends whose families share this practice are the Roman Catholic ones, but we're not RC.

High Rise – Long Drop

There's a rumour that our town is going to get its first skyscrapers – and they're going to be built next to what was my old school at Rising Brook. As it turns out these blocks of flats stop after the fifth floor. This is disappointing but they're still fairly impressive to play in while their construction continues. You can now get onto the roof of the first one. There's a really good view from there – you can see the castle.

When we get fed up of exploring the flats, we climb over the fence into the school field. Rising Brook is now a secondary school where the big kids go, and a vast new building is being constructed to house the new school hall. Already you can see where the stage is – and it's big. So, too, is the balcony with its wide, sweeping curve. No seats have yet been installed so you can run across or up-and down the tiers with little obstruction. It's possible to access the roof of this building, too. Unlike the flat tops of the flats, though, this has a slope which makes it more fun to mess about on.

None of us has yet fallen off or otherwise injured themselves at either of these places. This is more than can be said for the new Library which is under construction across the road. For some reason the scaffolding uprights soar way above the height of the roof that is now partly covered. They are great for climbing which is done in similar fashion to the rope-climbing we do at school. I'm looking across from the top of one of the poles and see Dave T quite high up another and still climbing. I don't know exactly how it happens but he suddenly plummets, making an unpleasant sound as he lands on the rubble way below. He's lying there with a gash to his leg and complaining about his right arm hurting a lot. There's a bloke passing by who I know slightly as a rep for Peekfreans, a biscuit firm connected in some way to the company my dad works for. He thinks Dave has broken his arm. In the absence of any handy material for a sling, he tries to get Dave to hold his arm against his own body with the hand pointing towards his chin. This seems to cause more pain so Mr Biscuit advises calling for an ambulance. As Dave's house is closer than the nearest phone box, he decides to go home first – and limps off, very slowly.

Doctor Frew

Our Doctor holds his surgery in a front room of his crumbling Georgian house in Tipping Street, just off the town centre. There's something about the room that I like. It's warm, quite cosy, and the medicinal smell of surgical spirit I find reassuring. It's an agreeable contrast to the open fire, brown linoleum floor and the old wood and leather of the Victorian furniture – the desk, the armed and staved chair on wheels and the horse-hair stuffed medical couch and matching sofa. The surgery is much more welcoming than the draughty, threadbare waiting room with the dirty curtains, where patients in damp overcoats sit on 1930s upright chairs trying to draw some benefit from the leaky, potentially lethal gas fire which barely flickers in the small grate. There is lino on the floor in this room, too, but it's thin, cracked and worn through in all the well-trodden bits.

The doctor himself is also reassuring – a bit like a Father Christmas without the beard. He does have a white moustache and hair, though, and a deep but gentle voice. His method of giving you injections, however, can be alarming. The way he holds his pen while writing prescriptions – the pen grasped between third and fourth fingers of an upturned and clawed right fist – is also that adopted when wielding the syringe. Steadying himself with his left hand by holding your arm just above the elbow, Dr Frew pauses with the end of the needle at least six inches away from your flesh. He then waits until the shaking in his right hand subsides sufficiently to suddenly plunge the pointy end of the hypodermic into your upper arm. Strangely, the discomfort I normally get from this unorthodox approach is no worse than from the jabs I've had in hospital or the vaccinations you get at school. Surprising, too, that in a man for whom the act of injecting appears to be physically difficult, it should be his treatment of choice. No matter whether you are suffering from an upset stomach, a bad rash or an outbreak of the lurgy, it seems you need an injection.

I do hear of one exception, however. Dad tells me of the time he asked Dr Frew to have a look at a strange lump on his wrist. As instructed, Dad lay his arm on the desk as the doctor examined the protrusion at close range. He seemed genuinely uncertain about a diagnosis as he reached for one of the heavy medical volumes on the bookshelf above his desk. While engaging in gentle chit-chat, and without warning, the book is smashed against Dad's wrist – and the ganglion disappears.

On this occasion, though, I'm tagging along with Dad who's here because my younger brother has earache. While the doctor considers the treatment, Dad lets slip that I'd also had the odd twinge in one of my ears but it's only mild. *Very* mild, I add, anticipating the inevitable form the treatment will take. Even so, Doctor F thinks it would be better if I had the injection as well to demonstrate to little brother that it doesn't hurt. So, I go first and, for some reason, this time it's a buttock, rather an arm, that is to take the punishment. And this time it does hurt.

As we leave, Dad points to this really filthy Morris Oxford of indeterminate colour parked on the street. He says it belongs to the doctor and that he never washes it. Instead, when the caked-on dirt and mud become so bad he can no longer see through the windscreen, he buys a new car.

Dad also tells me that Dr Frew had begun his medical training with the intention of becoming a surgeon. The First World War had intervened and he'd volunteered as one of the early fighter pilots. His career plans were altered after he was shot down over enemy territory sustaining severe burns and multiple other injuries. He was captured and became a prisoner of war. On repatriation to England he spent a long period in hospital before being declared unfit for further service. A permanent disability to his right hand was among the lasting effects of his horrific wounds.

A Christmas Amalgam

There are nine of us seated around the small dining table for Christmas Day dinner at Nan's. The main light is on even though it's early afternoon. My chair has a loose stave which I like to move up and down while I'm waiting for the turkey to be carved (a task allocated to Dad or Uncle Frank). Behind me the flaming log fire burns in the grate, spitting out the odd red cinder into the hearth or occasionally beyond the oak fender onto the rug. When this happens an adult puts their foot on it. On my right is the matching oak sideboard with its huge ornate-bordered mirror reflecting the Christmas tree in front of the window to my left.

The tree is in a pot on top of the wireless, next to the glass bowl in which Eb and Flo swim out their cramped existence. Eb is larger but Flo is a deeper orange. A few days ago I'd helped Mum to dress the tree, with the angel looking down at the coloured glass balls and tinsel. Each year we also hang a small spade, fork and rake – each in a different primary colour.

We eat the turkey with roast potatoes, mash, carrots, parsnip or swede, peas and gravy. The adults also eat sprouts. Bread sauce is on offer but Dad and I refuse (Dad calls it dog sick). Nan then brings in the large Christmas pudding which has been steaming up the window in the kitchen for hours. We are instructed to eat this carefully until we discover this year's lucky winner of the single silver joey that Nan has inserted inside. One Christmas the prize goes to me, at another it causes one of the adults to lose a filling. But this time no-one finds it; it's never seen again.

Tea is drunk with Christmas dinner. Except for the thimble of brandy used to ignite the pudding, Nan allows no alcohol in the house. During the meal Dad and Uncle Frank, with various excuses, absent themselves from the table for short periods of time – sometimes separately, occasionally together. I'm told by my older cousin that they seem to be interested in the large pockets of their overcoats which are hanging on the back of the kitchen door. He doesn't see what is contained therein but as the meal progresses these brief sojourns start to be accompanied by giggling and increasingly flushed faces as their owners return.

After dinner – while the adults do the washing-up or snooze in front of the fire – I go with John, my other cousin, round the corner to his house. This is good: with the place to ourselves we have an hour or two of freedom to do what we want. We go into the dining room so John can play a Chuck Berry record on his brother's gramophone and we decide to have a drink of Dandelion and Burdock. For some reason, John is shaking the pop bottle vigorously. The top shoots off and jets of the dark, sticky pop decorate the ceiling and walls and table and chairs and carpet and window and gramophone as they escape John's desperate attempts to stem the eruption. Our brief oasis of liberty turns abruptly to drudgery as we spend the time before the adults appear attempting to remove every trace of the offending liquid. This is not easy and, as far as the wallpaper is concerned, not even possible as stubborn and quite noticeable stains remain.

Plan B is therefore actioned as the adults arrive: keep them all out of the dining room. This proves not too difficult as our parents/aunts and uncles and grandmother either busy themselves in the kitchen with preparations for the Christmas tea or slump in front of the telly in the other room. As tea will be eaten while seated on the sofa and arm chairs of that room, there's a good chance that the new additions to the dining room décor will go unnoticed until tomorrow. By then, the cause and hence the culprits should be harder to discern.

My Father the Racing Driver

(1) "Don't tell your mother," says Dad as the Vauxhall Wyvern hurtles through country roads on our way back from a race meeting at Oulton Park. He points to the needle on the speedometer which can't go any further.

(2) Driving very fast down Yarlet Bank, father is pulled over by the police.
"Who do you think you are, Stirling Moss?"
"Yes."
Wrong answer.
Dad is booked for speeding.

Rag Day

'HOUSE FOR SALE 6d' declares the large whitewash lettering on the front gate of one of the grander detached residences. Dad and I spot this as we drive into town on Saturday morning. In the High Street the brass letter B has been removed from above the shop window of the long-established purveyor of over-priced gentlemen's clothing and school uniforms. It now reads 'ROOKFIELDS'. Dad explains the meaning of the word 'rook' when used as a verb. He says it's apt. I judge by his reactions that father rather approves of these Student Rag Day pursuits.

Arfoff and Alf

My Uncle Geoff cuts hair for a living and works for Harry Brown at his barber's shop in Marston Road. I hate going there because the smell of all the lotions and shampoos and hair creams makes my eyes stream. This reaction can be produced just walking past a hairdresser's.

So instead, my uncle cuts my hair at home – occasionally at his house but usually at ours. Every few weeks he arrives on his strange bicycle with his cutting kit – scissors, comb, hand clippers, cape – wrapped in brown paper and attached to the back of the saddle. He sits bolt upright on his bike, perhaps due to his time in the army but more likely because of the 'dropped' racing handlebars which he's inverted to an upwards position.

His method of working doesn't actually involve placing a basin on the top part of my head, – but the result isn't dissimilar. Not the most experimental of hair stylists, Geoff is reluctant to stray far from the standard short-back-and-sides of his training. As I get a bit older, my wish to try an alternative eventually wins the battle with my fear of the barber-shop and I venture once more into Harry Brown's hair emporium.

Things have changed, though. Harry Brown is no longer there having apparently suddenly and mysteriously disappeared, never to be seen again. My uncle also has left, swapping his haircutting career for a better paid job with the council. The shop is now owned and run by their more adventurous younger colleague, Alf Eley. He will still meet the requirements of the regulars, however, including the customer referred to by staff as Arfoff. At each hair appointment, he gives the same instruction: "I'll 'ave 'alf off, Alf."

But I'm there for a brush cut: similar to, but intended to be less severe than, a crew cut (Alf himself sporting a fine example of the latter). I watch apprehensively as more and more of my hair falls in layers down the cape and onto the floor. Through my watery eyes I just about discern in the mirror a haircut rather more in the image of Alf than I'd wanted, but I'm assured that he's left room for it to grow.

My mother pays for the haircut and, with the cool air assaulting my newly exposed scalp, we cross over the road to Ernie Green's post office. My gaze is still bleary from the aromas of Alf's shop and somehow the top of my head comes into sharp and painful contact with the corner of a metal display cabinet – containing safety advice leaflets. There is blood and someone supplies a sticking plaster. But there are reassurances, too, that my hair would soon grow, just as Alf had said.

How to Blag a Pit-side View

As our car edges closer to the front of the queue, Dad tells me to lie on the floor behind the front seats and Uncle Geoff leans over to cover me with their coats. They think the adult entrance fee for the motor cycle race meeting at Oulton Park is high enough already without having to buy a child's ticket as well.

Not only that, there is the additional expense of a car parking fee to avoid. They've come prepared. As Dad drives through to the parking area, I retake my place on the rear seat and Geoff takes the scissors to cut the top few inches off the front page of the *Daily Express*. Carefully folding the clipping, so that only the last five letters of the paper's name are displayed, he attaches it to the inside of the windscreen. We are waved through.

With that sorted, the next hurdle is the paddock. This is the best place to be before the races begin. It's where you can mingle with the likes of Scottish motor cycling ace Bob McIntyre or even 500cc world champion John Surtees, with his gleaming red MV Augusta, as they and their support teams prepare the bikes for the day's events. The paddock, though, is not easy to get into. You need a pass to enter – at least through the closely guarded entrance gate you do. Geoff spots a part of the temporary picket fencing some way away which is lying lower than the rest, having no doubt succumbed to repeated short-cuts to the tea tent. Dad picks up a couple of discarded empty bottles and, with the use of thumbs-up signs and other hand gestures, feigns communication with someone in the middle distance as the three of us step over the fence and we're in. The place is buzzing and I pull out my autograph book. Spoilt for choice, I'm unsure where to begin.

The races are due to start and, from the paddock, it's surprisingly easy to make the final breakthrough into the inner sanctum – the holiest of holy – the pits. A pit-side view is the most privileged of all. We just find a space – Pit 66 – and sit with our legs dangling over the counter-top, the start-and-finish line almost directly in front of us. In case of any future disbelievers, Dad is taking photos to prove it.

Bad News

When we play football it *is* normally 'jumpers for goalposts'. Jumpers have the advantage of being easily and infinitely movable to whichever patch of land we're using. Despite the cold and the wet, today we're playing at the corner of West Way and Somerset Road on a stretch of grass and (mainly) mud that's not yet been built on. The leather ball has become heavy as someone has forgotten to dubbin it, and there's a risk of lacerating your forehead with the soggy lace if you try to head it. It's a long match and the game goes on until dusk – and beyond. It's truly dark by the time I get home and I'm expecting a mild ticking-off for being late for tea. Instead, I'm met with long faces. Scraps of radio news are coming through about an air crash in Germany. A number of Manchester United players are thought to have died. United are the league champions and I know all the regular first team by name. I'm no longer feeling hungry.

Camping with Dad

Since the disastrous annual holiday a couple of years ago – when we had to come home early – my parents have not risked us all going away together. So this year, just Dad and I are going camping for a few days in Wales.

Dad's borrowed a largish green tent from the local Scout troop and we find a farmer who allows us to pitch it in one of his fields. We're near the village of Glan Conwy or, to give its full name, Llansanffraid Glan Conwy, meaning Church of St Ffraid on the Bank of the River Conwy. In fact, from our tent we have fine, far-reaching views over the estuary. The grass in the field is very long and very wet. We have a separate groundsheet, though, and we do our best to lay it over the uneven surface before moving in our bedding. This consists of two rudimentary camp beds, which we assemble, and a couple of blankets.

We're not permitted an open fire but Dad has brought a small primus stove which he gets going to brew some tea. We'd bought milk from the farmer when we first arrived. While we watched, he'd milked a cow and presented us with warm milk in a small pail. Horrible – it reminded me too much of the awful school stuff in third-pint bottles left stewing for hours beneath the rays of the sun – but Dad liked it.

We awake the first morning and count forty-nine dark hairy caterpillars on our blankets. It takes a while to prepare some breakfast, but eventually we set out for the day. We follow the river inland by driving just a few miles along the valley on the Llanrwst Road. A neighbour from home asked us to pay a visit to her relative. We find her in a lovely country cottage with a crystal-clear stream running through the sloping garden to the River Conway below. The banks of the stream are rocky and I'm fascinated by a small meshed door which opens outwards to reveal what I'm told is a meat safe – designed to keep its contents cool even in the warmest of weathers.

On the other side of the valley is a line of dark forbidding hills. Dad says that thirty-three years ago, after a fortnight of very wet weather, a dam burst releasing its contents down the steep incline and wiping out the village of Dolgarrog. Sixteen people died. Apparently, a lot of people were watching a film in the community hall on higher ground at the time the disaster struck, otherwise many more would have lost their lives. People locally still talk of the massive boulders washed down by the torrent and of cows left hanging from trees as the waters subsided.

I'm glad we are camping quite high up because it rains for much of the rest of our time away. This makes me compare it unfavourably with last year when Dad and I camped in another part of Wales, but in somewhat better weather. I recall that holiday quite clearly: I'm sitting on the passenger side of the front bench seat of the Vauxhall Wyvern, the black saloon car provided by Dad's employers, Huntley & Palmer's – the biscuit manufacturers. Dad's not that keen on the car – I don't think he likes the steering column gear change much – but it does go fast. And it's got a radio. The Everly Brothers are singing *Bye-Bye Love* as we round a bend – and there's the sea ahead of us. And here's our campsite to the left – well, a few tents pitched on the hills overlooking the bay to which we now add ours. Facilities are almost non-existent: there's a tiny green shed with barely room for the tin can with a lavatory seat on. We open the door… and immediately close it again. The smell is unbearable. "We won't be using this," Dad declares. He's an experienced camper used to a range of conditions, but I think even he has met his match with this one. There must be a water supply somewhere since Dad appears with our kettle ready for placing carefully on the small camp fire which he soon has roaring away. We're well into the evening by now and the sun is setting over the bay. I can see the dark shapes of Criccieth Castle cut into the red sky on the other side.

For the morning of our first full day, Dad suggests we go for a swim in the sea. By 'we' he means me. Because he had chronic mastoiditis as a child he never learnt to swim, but this made him all the more determined that I should learn. And since I have he's keen that I should use every opportunity to make use of the skill. Dad joins me in the water, though, but remains on his feet. Although the morning is warm and sunny, the sea is still very cold and after a couple of minutes I say I want to get out. Dad reluctantly agrees. We go to the King George IV Hotel in the High Street to make use of their posh toilets. Although it's too expensive to eat there every day, Dad says we can have one meal there – maybe this evening.

Dad seems rather subdued. I sense he's disappointed in me for cutting short the morning swim. So, later in the day I say I'd like another go. It's a gorgeous evening again and the water has warmed a little. The tide has been going out and is still receding, leaving hard ridges of sand. After swimming and paddling around in the shallows for a while, we start a knock-about with the hard red plastic football we've brought with us. Dad emits a short grunt of pain as he overestimates the depth of the water whilst attempting an almighty kick.

The next day, Dad's toe is a peculiar shape and it's turned black. He's hobbling a bit but that doesn't stop us driving into Porthmadog in the evening to see a film at The Coliseum cinema. We have seats in the circle. Before the start, some music is being played – a recording of the *Elizabethan Serenade*, a light musical composition by Ronald Binge. After the first airing, which lasts about three minutes, there's a bit of a gap and it's played again – and then a third time. The same occurs during the interval as the ice creams and lollies are sold to a few members of the sparse audience. It's obviously the only record the cinema possesses. During the main feature, the projector breaks down and it's three-quarters of an hour before it's up-and-running again. The delights of the *Elizabethan Serenade*, thinly spread to begin with, palled long ago this evening. But our ears continue to be assaulted by its repetitive strains which Dad says are now playing havoc with his digestive system. At the end of the film, and despite Dad's toe, we flee the circle and run downstairs chased by a final volley from Binge's orchestral infantry.

Our brief vacation is soon over but on the drive home I enjoy listening to music on the car radio. Until, that is, the opening bars of a familiar refrain are abruptly cut short with a sharp twist of the off knob. "Not that bloody music again!" mutters Dad as he replaces his left hand on the steering wheel. A day or two after we get back home, the doctor tells Dad his toe is broken. A lovely holiday nonetheless.

Dares

It's wrong to say children have no sense of danger. If they lacked this, they wouldn't dare each other to do risky things. Or perhaps that sense is outweighed by another.

On the Wolverhampton Road, before you get to Rowley Bank, a replacement bridge is under construction over the main LMS London Euston to Glasgow railway line. At the top, next to the footpath, the brickwork to the pillars has been completed but the railings between them are yet to be installed. On each pillar, at a little above pavement level, is the narrowest of parapets that slopes downward a little. We dare each other to circumvent the first pillar. With some difficulty and a lot of concentration, it can be done. It's just possible to stretch out your arms far enough to get a bit of a grip at the sides of the pillar's width. With little more than toes on the parapet, you can then edge cautiously all the way round and back to the safety of the pavement. From the other three sides you know there is a long drop onto the piles of builders' rubble at the edge of the tracks. Best not to look down.

Why do we do it? No bets accompany the dare. Money is not changing hands. But there's a terrific sense of achievement when you accomplish the task – and you've survived. We've heard from fellow trainspotters on the Crinoline footbridge that some kids have been playing chicken on the railway lines. That's plain stupid. Some of us may have gone so far as standing on the iron parapet there to disappear in the clouds of thick smoke as the trains rattle beneath, but there are limits.

Skylark and Lilac

I'm lying in the soft slope of the clover meadow near the top of our road. There are buttercups, too. But all I'm seeing now are the blue sky and the few lines of high wispy cloud as I squint upwards through the distorted rays of the sun.

There is someone next to me but we don't speak and there is no movement. I'm aware that what I'm experiencing has happened once before. It's my earliest memory. I'm lying on my back in the pram beneath the lilac tree in blossom. On the breeze I catch its sweetness. Today, though, it's not a scent but a sound that is drawing my attention. It's the sound of a skylark. I don't see it but I know it is hovering way above, waiting for that moment it will drop to its nest on the ground.

The feeling is not exactly happiness. It's gentler: less exuberant, more serene. I think it's called contentment.

Cousins Taking Advantage

I have this large ball of silver paper which I started from scratch by screwing up the inner wrapper of a bar of chocolate. I've been adding to it with more pieces for what seems like years. There's a girl called Susan who visits our house very occasionally. I'm told she is my cousin but unlike my other cousins I rarely see her. She comes with Uncle Geoff but she doesn't live at his house as he lives alone. She finds my precious silver ball and I tell her how I've made it. She starts to unwrap it, piece by piece, layer by layer, pausing every so often to gauge my reaction. I desperately want her to stop but think it would be impolite to say so. Eventually, the floor and settee are abundantly littered with the shiny fragments of my endeavours. The silver ball is no more.

Any of my other cousins would have been told to pack it in and, if they didn't, I would forcibly try to stop them. There can be exceptions even here, though. Cousin John has just come out of hospital after months of extensive and painful treatment following a horrendous accident at his home. He'd almost burnt to death after attempting to enliven the living room fire with a generous application of paint thinners. He's called round with his mum and has taken a shine to my lovely, recently acquired Derringer pistol.

"How much do you want for this?" asks John.

"Two shillings," I say, thinking that such an exorbitant sum would put him off the idea.

"Done!"

Oh bugger. I'd overlooked the fact that during his lengthy spell in the infirmary he's accumulated a healthy sum of unspent pocket money which is now bursting his pockets. To make matters worse, I feel pangs of guilt about taking his money after all he's been through – and I say he can have the gun for nothing. Double bugger.

"Thanks, Dave," he says, taking charge of his new toy. "And can I have that box of caps to go with it?"

The Floating Cap (1)

It's Saturday morning and my parents are standing tall, holding a letter. They are trying hard to give me a serious telling-off but are not being very successful. Dad, in particular, seems to be having difficulty in keeping his face straight. The letter is from my headteacher and it will mark the end of a brief but entertaining end-of-school-day activity that a friend and I had invented a week or so ago.

Each afternoon we've been removing a couple of items from the lost-property box in the cloakroom – a scarf, glove, the odd plimsoll, that sort of thing – and taking them down the footpath to the little bridge over the stream. To the amusement of any other kids in the vicinity we then drop them into the water before rushing to the other side to see them emerge beneath us and float onwards downstream.

I think I know how we got rumbled. On Wednesday, Alan Beard is laughing along with the rest of us as an upside-down school cap begins its watery travels – until he recognises the fancy name-tag his mum has sewn in.

Apparently I'm now to make a weekly contribution from my pocket-money as recompense for various articles of missing clothing listed in the letter. I wonder how my friend is faring with his parents.

The Generous Dentist

I have toothache and my usual dentist is on holiday so Dad has taken me to another place in town. I'm in there for no more than twenty minutes. During this time I'm treated to six fillings, five of which are completely unnecessary. I don't discover this until much later when I read that cases of 'Aussie trench' are not uncommon among baby-boomers. All you need is a crazy system for remunerating practitioners and a greedy bastard of a dental surgeon who doesn't give a toss about permanently weakening the hitherto pristine gnashers of trusting children. And I wasn't even given any anaesthetic!

But to name the practice by reference to one nationality seems rather a slur on our Antipodean dental cousins. It would be odd if they have been the only ones ripping off the National Health Service in this way. The dentist who has been so generous with the amalgam in my mouth, for example, is as English as Terry Thomas.

Another Brick Removed

The period following the war and continuing through the 1950s is turning out to be the best ever for my team, the great Wolverhampton Wanderers FC. I've therefore never known a situation when Wolves have been anything other than a top team. There have been only two seasons when they've not finished in the top six of the First Division.

Unfortunately, the same cannot be said of my dad. He's unable to hide his disappointment each time he shows me the regional Huntley & Palmers Sales Rep Performance league tables. Invariably, he's languishing in the lower realms. He tells me about the pressure from his bosses to employ harder sales tactics. "What's the point?" says Dad, "Most of my clients are small shopkeepers. If I persuade them to buy more than they need one month, they'll only reduce their order the next." Once I shove aside the image of tiny overalled people barely able to see over their shop counters, I can see Dad's predicament and feel sorry for him. He's in the wrong sort of job. People are far more important to him than biscuits. I don't view his 'failure' to hit sales targets as any failing on his part – the opposite, in fact. I feel pleased and quite grown-up that he feels able to share his frustrations with me.

I felt far less comfortable on the occasion Dad unintentionally revealed another type of vulnerability. It's a few years ago, probably during one of his religious phases, and he's taken me to church with him. The service hasn't yet started and we've barely sat down when, without warning, Dad drops to his knees. His hands are together, elbows on the prayer book shelf on the back of the pew in front. He closes his eyes tightly and the lips are moving slightly in what I suppose is silent prayer. I'm truly shocked. More than that I'm confused and distressed. I've not seen father like this before. In my eyes, Dad is the source of all knowledge and wisdom. He's the invincible one and beholden to nobody. But here he is, showing weakness and deferring to some greater power than himself. I think, above all, I feel suddenly unprotected.

I soon get over it. I suppose it's just a part of growing up, another brick removed from the wall of childhood innocence.

Empty Vessels

It's a favourite saying of our teacher which she uses to admonish noisy pupils. "Empty vessels make the most noise," she says. The fact that she's always saying it shows it's not working. So she's giving us a visual – and auditory – demonstration. She has two jars with lids on. One has two small stones in; the other is crammed full of them. She shakes them in turn. "Which one makes the most noise?" she asks.

We're supposed to say the first one. But this is stupid. Neither of the jars is empty: they both have stones in.

We Come Along on Saturday Morning

There could be three, four or five of us, depending on who turns up each time. We rehearse our act on the steps at the hall end of the playground, usually to an adoring audience of two or three girls from the year below. We're a boy band except we never use the 'b' word as 'bands' are associated with squares and uncool oldies such as Billy Cotton and Joe Loss. We are a vocal group and we perform each Saturday morning on stage at the Odeon Club, before the films start.

Our repertoire consists of rock 'n' roll numbers, mainly those sung by Elvis Presley and Buddy Holly. We're accompanied by Jumbo Judson on the piano. Apparently he's a teacher at the grammar school. He usually doesn't know the songs we're about to do but asks us to start and he'll "pick it up as we go along".

We seem to go down OK. We're not booed (as the baddies in today's cowboy film will be) and we're now even getting recognised on the bus going home. The manager seems to like us, too, as he's invited us to a meeting in his office after school on Monday. He has an interesting proposal to put to us, he says. On our way back we wonder what he might mean. Perhaps he wants to manage us? We've heard of people like Larry Parnes, taking unknown singers and turning them into stars.

When we get there on the Monday we have to wait for ages. He seems busy and preoccupied, shoves some sheet music into our hands, saying this is what he wants us to sing on Saturday, and bundles us out. On the pavement outside, we look at the sheets he's pressed on us. *Tulips From Amsterdam. You Need Hands.* Bloody Max Bygraves songs! Not on your bleeding nelly, and various versions of similar sentiments are shared among ourselves. We won't be doing that stuff.

So, that's the end of our weekly Odeon sessions, and also the end of the group – well almost. We remember that the talent competition is only a few weeks away so decide to get together for one final occasion. But musical differences are racking the group from within. We can't agree on choice of number.

I quit the group and enter the competition as a solo act, singing Buddy Holly's *Oh Boy!* I think I'm singing more or less in tune but there's a problem looming. I've started in too high a key and I know I'm not going to reach the high note with the last syllable of 'toni-ight'. Only one thing for it: drop an octave for that one note.

The competition is judged by the volume of audience reaction. I don't win, but get a wallet as second prize. It looks a bit like leather but is probably plastic. The winner is… the rest of the group I've just left. At least I did better than the three girls dressed as windmills singing *Tulips From* bloody *Amsterdam*, despite their support from the lone bout of enthusiastic applause from someone in the wings.

The Great Mangold Swindle

The farmer says he'll pay us 2/6d an hour or, and with a gesture to what we see are relatively short rows, five shillings a row for mangold weeding. The latter, we're informed, would require less supervision. This, the piece-rate, seems a much better proposition, which we agree to accept.

Taking a row each, it's only after almost an hour of solid graft that we reach the top of the incline – and stare in disbelief as each row now stretches before us into the distance. We've been done!

The only consolation is that I, and a couple of the others, have only just worked out what a mangold looks like, so have been weeding rather indiscriminately. And Rob has been operating in the belief that mangold weeding means just that – weeding the mangolds and leaving all other growth intact.

Memorable Moments at Molineux

I've seen wonderful matches at Molineux. No doubt there have been poor ones, too, but you tend to forget those. It helps if there are goals, preferably in the opposing team's net, but goals are not always essential for memorable games. One of the best I've witnessed was a 0–0 draw with West Ham. Floodlights on, a teeming cowshed end, thunderous support from the cheers and the rhythmic stomping of feet on the wooden tiers of terraces high in the stands behind me. It's the atmosphere that makes it. Normally there's a tremendous feel to the place: the air of expectation before the game; checking the teams in the programme and buying a couple more sixpenny badges of players to add to my woolly hat; the good-natured teasing of the opposing fans outnumbered in the unsegregated crowd; the roar greeting the teams as the two sides run out onto a (sometimes) pristine pitch.

There can be the odd scary moment. At the first big game my dad takes me to, the South Bank is so packed that an almighty crush forms as fans funnel towards the narrow exit. The parental hand gripping my upper arm is not there anymore. And I become aware that my feet are no longer in contact with the ground as a wave of movement in the crowd is sending me hurtling towards a brick wall. The seemingly inevitable collision is averted when I'm plucked from danger and deposited on someone's shoulders. The shoulders belong to Dad. He'd somehow managed to reach across and effect a last-second rescue.

Then there's the occasion when our whole section of the crowd is detained for ages after the Blackburn Rovers game because someone has been seriously wounded in a stabbing on the terraces. Or – less nasty but still a bit hairy – the time two of us are chased through West Park by disappointed

Liverpool fans. They don't even stop as we jump onto our waiting transport. They run us up the stairs until they see the top deck full of the old gold and black and thirty heads turning to see what the kerfuffle is about. Observing a few wearers of alien scarves tumbling over themselves while attempting a speedy backward descent down the twisty staircase of a Midland Red bus does make for a rather heart-warming spectacle. Especially when performed to a chorus of loud cheers and associated gesticulations.

The mood for this afternoon's match is good. The ground is already crammed to capacity. Wolverhampton Wanderers and today's opponents, Manchester United, are the two most successful post-war teams in England. Since the Munich air crash, Man United have gained an even bigger following nationally, and there's a fair bit of red-and-white on the terraces. Their fans are still a minority though, as the colourfully deafening crescendo when Wolves score clearly demonstrates. The pair-upon-pair of arms reaching to the heavens, the manic bouncing up and down and the ecstatic scarf-waving all contribute to the seethe and surge of mass elation sweeping the ground. But it's the sounds, too: the shouts, the delighted clapping, and the machine-gun rapidity of a thousand football rattles energetically spun, mine included.

That is until I'm left holding the stump of a handle as the main part of my machine – with the rattle blades alternately painted black and orangey-yellow and with tassels attached to the cog end – abruptly launches above the heads of some younger fans. The velocity of its departure ensures a considerable distance is covered in no time. Ahead is the head of a large man. It takes a direct hit and turns angrily to seek the culprit. Please let it not belong to a Man U fan! The glowering face clocks the frightened kid with the small piece of wood in his still-raised hand. But it unfolds as the man registers my colours, and it turns into a grin as he rubs the back of his head.

'Phew,' as they say in the Beano.

Helping Cousin with Paper Round

I'm helping Brian, my cousin four years older, with his after-school paper round. He's been doing it for a while and is familiar with his customers' individual quirks and requirements. He points to a house in Coronation Road and tells me a severely disabled woman lives there. As it takes her a long time to reach the front door, he advises me on the mode of delivery. I'm to roll-up her copy of the *Express & Star* and insert it half-way through her eye-level letter-box before administering a hard whack to propel it as far as possible down her hallway. I'll then probably hear a grateful 'thank-you' as she retrieves the paper to read in her kitchen.

I carry out his instructions. But instead of any expression of gratitude, I hear the sound of crashing glassware, a rapidly opened front door and the appearance of a very angry and surprisingly agile lady who chases me down her front garden and along the street. Meanwhile, cousin Brian is nowhere to be seen – until the squeaks and wheezes of uncontrollable laughter direct me around the corner to the crouching figure behind the hedge.

My Collections

I've collected a lot of different things since I was little. Shiny beach pebbles, lapel badges worn proudly on my very first school blazer, football cards from cigarette, tea and bubblegum packets, bottle tops, programmes from football matches and motor race meetings, marbles with unusual colourings or patterns – these are some of the more common ones. I'm now into cigarette packets. I love the retained smell of the tobacco as I remove the silver paper and inner carton before cutting out the fronts to stick them in the scrapbook. I start with the more obvious brands – Player's Navy Cut and Senior Service from Dad, or the empty packs of Woodbines, Park Drive or Player's Weights which you can pick up in the street or from any waste bin – before progressing to the more attractive or rarer designs of those cadged from older friends. These bigger lads, a year or two our seniors, spend their pocket money or paper-round wages on whatever catches their eye in the local shop. Churchill Number Ones seem rather posh and the corked-tipped Craven A, advertised as harmless for your throat, are added to the collection, as are Capstan Full Strength, Piccadilly and Kingsway with the new bright red flip-top pack. Sometimes these boys will let you have a drag of their smokes. The really exotic fags – like Passing Cloud, Sobranie Black Russian or the boxes of their pastel-shaded cocktail cigarettes – are the most sought after. A spare one of these can be swapped for three or four of the more mundane packets. Some of the older boys will swear that their latest brand of ciggy is the best yet by far, but once alight they all seem the same to me. I've not yet learned to inhale but I can blow smoke out of my nose and this is where I can taste them the most.

Bo Jollis and Sex

Mum's back from work and discovers me asleep in the space between the fireplace and the damp washing on the clothes horse. I'd got soaked through on my way home from school and had been trying to prise some warmth from the dying embers in the grate.

Having worked for a while at Woodhall's the

haberdashers ('the best place in town to get felt'), Mum now has a part-time job a few doors down from there at Timothy White's & Taylor's, just off the Market Square. Returning to a cold house on a day like this is about the only downside of no-one being home when I get back. Most days I quite like having the house to myself for a while. I retrieve the door key from the little ledge above the garage door and decide how I shall occupy myself for the next hour or so.

I might spread a thick coating of butter on a crust of bread. If more adventurous, I'll prepare a sliced apple and sugar sandwich. Or I'll explore places I'm not supposed to – such as the large and ugly walnut-veneered wardrobe in the parental bedroom. At the foot of the big section is a bottle of what Dad calls Bo Jollis. It has a broken cork stuffed in the top. The contents diminish over time, but incredibly slowly. My parents don't like it. They say it tastes like vinegar. It does, I've tried it. It was brought back from a trip to France by Uncle Geoff.

In one of the top parts there's a very thick book wrapped in multiple layers of brown paper. On the outer sheet is written 'To Ray & Joan from Auntie Eva & Uncle Tom'. Eva and Tom are my Nan's neighbours and are strict Baptists (well, at least Eva is. I suspect Tom tags along for a quiet life). I'm pretty sure they would not have bought the book – it will be the wrapping from some other gift – because the title is *The Encyclopaedia of Sexual Knowledge*. It's a very interesting book which I dip into from time to time so by the age of eleven I've a fair knowledge of the subject – at least in theory.

Once, Twice, Three Times a Halfwit

If once is an incident and twice coincidence then how to account for the third?

The first occasion is during one of our oological excursions. We're not like some kids who find a bird's nest and steal all the eggs from it. We never take more than one egg at a time. Pete's the expert egger so we usually end up at his place where he blows away the egg's innards after making holes at each end. (And it *is* blowing, not sucking as pal Martin once discovered.) The shell is then added to our collection. The hedgerows along Barn Bank Lane are a good place for birdnesting and today we find quite a few. The eggs include the brown speckled greenish-blue of the blackbird and the plainer but more striking blue of the hedge sparrow. We place the day's cache carefully into the little saddlebag of the borrowed bike I'm using and head off down the narrow country lane. Towards the bottom of the first hill I skid on some gravel and collide with John C's bike. I fall onto the grassy bank at one side of the road but John comes off worse and thinks he's broken his wrist. We hear an approaching motor so the rest of us pull the bikes to the sides. We see it's an ambulance. It slows down as it gets near so we point to John, visibly in pain sitting at the roadside opposite. The driver looks but doesn't stop. He squeezes his vehicle between us, it picks up speed and is soon out of sight over the brow of the hill. We look at each other in perplexed disappointment. Is this not an emergency? I collect my bike. Not a single egg remains unbroken.

Another day. Another year. I'm building up quite a speed on the descent at Pear Tree Bank. As I'm sitting at the side of the road, dazed, grazed and gingerly holding a bleeding hand against my bruised and rapidly swelling right cheekbone, my mate Logs is telling me I've just had a speed wobble. He describes my airborne trajectory over the handlebars before I land on one side of the road with my bike coming to rest by the old milestone on the other. One of the newer-version hospital wagons whizzes past, apparently oblivious to Logs' attempts to wave it down.

It's hard to believe that there could be a third such boy-bicycle-emergency vehicle combination, but there is. I'm on my way through Highfields estate for a makeshift game of footie. And on this occasion there can be no doubt that the ambulance staff clearly witness my mishap since it plays out directly in front of them. I see their vehicle travelling towards me in the second before the net containing my ball gets caught in the front wheel. Again, it's an over-the-handlebar number but this time it's the ribs that take the worst battering as I make awkward contact with the high concrete curb. And, once again the ambulance speeds its way onwards without the hint of a pause. This time, however, the warning bells and flashing headlamps could explain the lack of concern for a careless young halfwit on a bike.

Damp Day Out

It's a predicament requiring immediate resolution. The method of resolution depends on a snap either/or decision. With one foot on the island, the other on the stern of the rowing boat, I realise our mooring is a little on the slack side. As the one foot gracefully departs its neighbour and I'm threatened with the sharp pain of an unintended yet imminent gymnastic manoeuvre, do I throw myself to the safety of land or leap onto the boat?

I choose the former. Unfortunately I'm not quite successful. Momentarily both feet are safely planted, but I feel myself falling backwards, a movement my flapping arms can't correct. The water at Trentham Lake is surprisingly deep at that spot. Once he's stopped snorting like a pig with a fresh bucket of swill, Johnnie C says I was completely submerged for a few seconds. I've rarely seen such unruly laughter and JC is still doubled-up and pointing to the watery place from which I've now emerged.

We manage to get a bit of a fire going. It's a chilly afternoon and I'm wearing nothing but a cycle cape as we attempt in vain to dry my clothes. When we're about to leave the island, I ask Johnnie what could be worse than putting on damp, soggy pants, jeans and shirt in today's weather and with the prospect of a fifteen-mile bike ride home ahead of us. "Oh, there's plenty," he replies as I get into the boat, carefully.

A Reluctant Scholarship Boy

The one thing that really matters to me is football. After school, at weekends and through the school holidays playing football is all I want to do. It's what I live for. So, when the letter that seemingly everyone has been waiting for drops through the letterbox, it's of little interest to me. Addressed to my mum and dad it says I have been allocated a place at Stafford's King Edward VI School, the town's only grammar school for boys.

I remind my parents of the deal we struck a few months ago when I sat what is commonly if not officially referred to as the 11+ Exam. In Staffordshire it takes the form of four tests, held over a couple of days, the results of which largely determine the type of schooling each pupil is offered from the age of eleven. In our part of the country this means a place at either secondary grammar school for a minority judged to be of 'academic aptitude and ability' or a secondary modern school for everyone else. It's not supposed to be a pass/fail exam, but that's how it's seen by the vast majority of kids, their parents and teachers. Some people even still talk of 'winning a scholarship'.

I don't care what it's called because I've already decided which school I'll be going to. Whatever the outcome of the tests, I intend to opt for the default position – the local sec mod. I've heard that because football – proper Association Football – is regarded as too much a working-class game for snotty King Edward Grammar, it is not allowed. Instead they play something called Rugby Union. At Rising Brook Secondary Modern, on the other hand, football is more than tolerated, it's positively encouraged. On match days there are proper nets on the goalposts and everything.

All this I explain to my parents. Since I've no intention of going to the grammar school even if I have the chance, there's no point in my being bothered at all, as many kids are, by the tests. Mum and Dad listen sympathetically to all this and then suggest that, just out of interest, I do the best I can at the tests but promise that if I am then offered a place at grammar school and still don't want to go they'll abide by my decision. That seems fair enough so I do as they propose – hence my reminder now that the letter has arrived. And, with no attempt to persuade me otherwise, my parents stick to their word and confirm that, in the end, the choice is mine.

What happens over the next few days I do not expect. Final year pupils arriving at our primary school next morning are confronted by a group of excited girls demanding to know if we've 'passed'. Teachers are giving out congratulations or commiserations as they deem appropriate. Some pupils are in tears. Too much fuss. But there's worse to come. I start to receive laudatory comments and cards from grandparents, aunts and uncles, friends of the family, even neighbours. Many of these are accompanied by money – and often paper money: the ten shilling and one-pound notes are mounting up to a tidy sum.

This presents me with a dilemma. How to I tell all these well-meaning people I'm not going to accept the offer of this school place? Or am I now under a moral obligation to go the bloody grammar school after all? And, if I don't, will I have to return all this cash even though mentally I've already spent it?

I should add that my mum and dad are still holding to their side of the deal. There's no pressure from them and they haven't given me money nor even a card. And, unlike many of my friends, I never received the pre-tests bribe of a new bike if I passed the 11+. I feel rather proud of them for their stance. Perhaps with this in mind, I'm persuaded, again just out of interest, to attend the information evening held in King Edward VI School hall. It's there, later this evening, that I finally agree to my dad signing away the next five years of my life.

At times, parents can be very adept at the long game.

The First Day

Some kids – perhaps most – have it far worse on their first day at KESS (as the school is not affectionately known). There are those first-years who get their heads thrust into a not-always-particularly clean toilet bowl while the contents of the overhead cistern are discharged with a gleeful tug of the chain. It is not uncommon for this initiation ceremony to be performed multiple times upon the same boy. There is no organization behind the rituals. Newbies are seized at random from the playground by marauding ganglets of older boys and protestations that "I've been done already," cut no ice even if the soggy hair and damp shoulders display pretty clear evidence that it's true.

I'm one of the lucky ones. A couple of second-years, out to avenge the maltreatment they no doubt received twelve months ago, march me not to the school bogs but to the far more acceptable environs of the Hanging Rooms. So called because the letter 'C' has long since disappeared from the door, these inter-connected rooms contain the showers, fixed benches and clothing pegs plus the entire school complement of pupil-use washbasins. It is in one of these that I undergo my one – and only – ducking. My duckers are surprisingly considerate. After inserting the plug, the cold and the hot taps are both turned on – whether to take off the chill or to complete the sink-filling more quickly I'm not sure – and my head is held underwater for just a second or two.

Relieved that my investiture has been less traumatic than expected, I start to dry my hair on the damp and manky roller towel when my initiators are grabbed by a group of third-year boys. They now find themselves bent forwards over the cracked sanitary ware as their heads are submerged in adjacent basins. It is punishment for bullying younger boys, they are told, and they don't receive the luxury of any hot water in their sinks. Two of the older group are from our neighbourhood and have always been quite friendly towards me and my mates. I half expect the door to burst open once again and for my Samaritans in turn to be subject to the summary justice of fourth-years. But the chain of retribution stops here. They wander off and I experience no further attentions of a baptismal nature.

What Do You Want?

Adam Faith is singing *What Do You Want* again. According to Mum it's for the umpteenth time today. How many is that? It's the very first record I have bought because until last week we've never had a gramophone. Uncle Geoff is moving house and he's given us his old radiogram. It's very large – Mum calls it a monstrosity – and rather takes over the living room. We've had to move the budgie's cage on its stand to the other side of the room so we can fit it in between the hearth and the dining table.

77

Geoff's also passed on his record collection – mainly big band, jazz and guitar music and some humorous ones too – but most are quite old. There's a few I'm quite fond of – Spike Jones & His City Slickers, and the Les Paul stuff, for example. I also like the alliterative Big Ben Banjo Band but for the name rather than their music. And there's a couple of Elvis records, including *Jailhouse Rock* that my cousin Nina must have bought to play when visiting her father. She doesn't live with my Uncle Geoff – until she married a few years ago she always lived with our Nan and Grandad. They don't have a gramophone or a television but I doubt Grandad would allow the playing of any records unless they were by Paul Robeson. I think *The Man From Laramie* is also one of Nina's. Something has happened to the hole in the centre and it's now more of an oval. When you play it, Jimmy Young's voice undulates severely in pitch which makes me laugh at the long notes.

I want to build my own collection, though, and it's Adam Faith that kicks it off. I've had to buy the 78rpm version. Most singles are now sold in the new much smaller 'unbreakable' 45rpm format but our gramophone will only play 78s – at least officially. After a while I find a – not entirely satisfactory – way of getting round the problem, and coincidentally it's pop-star Adam who helps with this. Inside the gramophone I discover a mechanism that adjusts the speed of the turntable. I've heard that *What Do You Want* is one of the shortest records ever released, lasting only one minute thirty-five seconds. I borrow a 45 version of the song from a friend, together with some other singles. The speed control has no set gradations so, using trial and error, the second hand of my watch and multiple playings of Mr Faith's ditty (which is now driving my mum up the wall, she says), I eventually get the play time down to an exact one minute thirty-five.

That's OK. But it does leave problems. There's the fuss of repeatedly having to reverse the process each time I want to switch between 45s and 78s (particularly the first time when I have to apply my meagre mathematical skills). Then there's the pick-up arm: it's far too heavy for the lighter 45s. It does play them but my friend claims it's caused them damage and refuses to lend me any more. On top of all that is the advice to change the needle of the pick-up head after every record. It's not difficult to do but, compared with the modern record players, it becomes an irritating, time-consuming hassle. Besides, you can quickly get through a little tin box of replacement needles (available from Harold E Parkes' shop in St Mary's Passage) and they cost 2/– a time. All in all, you can see why I head my fantasy Christmas-wish list with a Dansette record player. I should be so lucky!

School Rules: Problems and Solutions

The preamble to the School Rules of King Edward VI Grammar School for Boys begins with two highly contestable propositions: *School rules are few in number and clearly defined...* and these are followed immediately with a stern warning: *...infringement of them is punishable; and a plea of ignorance is not accepted as an excuse.*

Rule 3. All boys must wear the school cap and an official school tie on school days in the town, travelling to or from School or School games, when representing the School and at School functions. The School uniform is a school blazer with grey flannels; boys in the lower school wear shorts, unless permission for long trousers is given. Pullovers are V-necked, grey or navy in colour, shirts are plain white or grey, socks plain and sober in colour, and shoes black, of the round-toed Oxford type.

Problem. It is never explained just what an Oxford-type shoe is.

Solution. Persuade shoe-buying parent that the would-be winkle-picker or chisel-toe footwear in Curtis' window falls within the permitted definitional parameters. Then wait until a teacher spots you wearing them and suggest it would be unfair to expect my parents to be able to buy another pair seeing as they've just forked out a princely sum on the fashionable items I'm currently sporting. If this fails, come to school in the tattiest pair of old pumps you can lay your hands on and feet into until teacher relents.

Rule 6. Boys who remain to dinner must eat their meal in the Dining Hall; the School authorities cannot be held responsible for the safety of boys who leave the school premises during the dinner hour.

Problem. Our school meals do not enjoy the best of reputations, as summed up in the frequently heard ditty, sung to the tune of *Out of Town* from the 1956 film Charley Moon:

Say what you will
School dinners make you ill
Though you do your best to keep them down.
Our school din-dins
Come from pig bins
Out of town.

Solution. Ask parents to provide you with sandwiches. Better still, persuade them that the food provided at school is so bad you can't possibly eat it so it would be better to spend the money in a cafe in town. The latter carries the added bonus of legitimately evading Rule 6 and thus allowing a wide range of out-of-school alternatives. A favourite of mine is to buy a few penny stale cakes from Jaspers, across the road from the school, leaving enough over for a pack of five Woodbines. Sometimes I'll substitute a bag of chips for the cakes. My mate JT often has even more to spend on the ciggies by smuggling a can of baked beans from the pantry at home. He'd then eat these – cold and out of the can – for his lunch. One winter's day, he comes across a deserted but still burning workmen's brazier and enjoys the luxury of heated beans for a change.

Rule 11. All punishment work must be done in special books allotted for the purpose at School during afternoon detention… There is a detention on Saturday mornings for more serious offences, and the boys entered for this cannot be excused except by special leave from the Head Master.

Problem. Following customer complaints of late deliveries of their copies of the *Express & Star*, I will eventually lose my paper round job because of too many late afternoon detentions.

Solution. It might be argued that staying out of trouble would avoid detentions. With so many rules and so many masters, school prefects and even low-status house prefects able to dish out detention 'pages' at will, this is far easier said than done. It's rumoured that some boys have been able to persuade the Headmaster to negotiate a caning in place of a Saturday morning detention, but I'm not convinced of the wisdom or desirability of such a swap. Otherwise, there is virtually no way out of serving time on a Saturday morning: the Head is known for his incorruptibility and insensitivity to bribery.

Rule 12. No boy may bring fireworks, explosives, or dangerous weapons to school.

Well, I'm glad I've read this or I would never have known such items are discouraged. It makes my parents wonder when and why it was thought necessary to include such a rule. What has been going on that school? Are they having second thoughts about sending their son there?

Rule 16. *Boys are not expected to be out in the streets late at night; it is not desirable that boys should attend evening amusements during term time except at week-ends.*

Problem. What about going to Youth Club or if there's a good film on at the cinema or just hanging about with your mates?

Solution. Just ignore this one. The chances of bumping into a teacher at night are low. Just occasionally we come across the odd one coming out of a pub in town, but he's normally too drunk to care… or remember.

Rule 18. *The School has first claim on the time of boys who are chosen to play for School or House teams.*

Problem. Arguably the most unfair rule of all, this has the potential for interfering in boys' other activities far too much. Rather to my surprise, I find I'm not too bad at rugby and am selected to play for the Under-13s. Some of the games against other schools are played on a Saturday. This is a serious problem as it means I'm not available to play for my football team.

Solution. I decide to start playing badly at rugby practice. I don't like doing this and find it difficult. But pride comes second to my need to play proper football, and after just a few games I'm dropped from the school team and Saturday afternoons once more belong to me and my football team.

As Hard as Nails

Before introducing to us to neck-springs from the wooden vaulting box, the PE teacher takes our little group on a tour of chalk-circled blood-spots on the gym floor. "This is what happened to the last pupils who tried this," he explains with relish. He has the same ghoulish look on his face as when splashing the iodine on open wounds from gymnasium or sports field accidents.

Such injuries are quite frequent. It's as if activities are selected according to the degree of pain they are likely to inflict. Our gym teacher does seem to derive enjoyment from it all. A favourite game we are required to play at least once a term is Murder Ball. "It's a special treat," he says, but for whom we are not told. The class is divided into two groups who face each other and a heavy medicine ball is placed in the centre. The object of the game is for each team to get the ball onto the opposing team's gym mat at the end of the room. There is only one rule: no kicking – of the ball. Otherwise, pretty much any method of preventing your opponents getting the ball through your half is permissible.

The teacher reckons he's toughening us up to make men of us. He's keen to emphasise just how tough he is personally.

"How hard am I?" he asks, to which we are expected to chant in unison: "As hard as nails."

"As hard as nails what?"

"As hard as nails, *sir*."

I've noticed, though, what seems to be a reluctance on his part to get involved directly when it comes to demonstrating new exercises or routines. He prefers to demonstrate his manly prowess through the threat – and use – of physical punishments, and with the aid of sports equipment including a size 12 gym shoe and a cricket bat called *Killer*. Add to that the permanent, lip-curling snarl that fronts the five-o-clock shadow, and you get an idea of the menacing presence that accosts us fresh-faced first-years each PE lesson.

According to some of the older boys in the school, this ultra-macho stance stems from a deep-seated inferiority complex. At morning assembly in the school hall he is the only teacher without an academic gown. Unlike all the others he is not a university graduate, his unadorned checked sports jacket standing out like a sore thumb on the stage each day.

A Metaphorical Riposte

Mr Newman (English teacher): "Roberts, give me an example of a metaphor."

"You are a pig, sir."

Sir gives me a longish, knowing look.

I respond in kind, with an added small but tight-lipped grin.

Are You All Turds?

There's a new teacher in school (or 'master' as we are supposed to refer to them). He approaches a group of us in the playground and asks, "Are you all turds?" We glance at each other with bemused looks, but none of us answers because it seems such a strange thing to ask. Is this man trying to insult us? He doesn't look as though he is: his expression telling of a genuine enquiry. He asks exactly the same question again, his face a little redder. He says something else from which we gather he has a strong accent, and then some of us guess that he is asking if we are all third-formers, or 'thirds', as we're known. Thirds are in fact first-year pupils (for reasons connected with the school's long history). We're not sure what the accent is but, after he moves on to confuse some other boys, we have a discussion about it. The shortest odds are on Welsh.

This seems to be confirmed a couple of days later when I have a second encounter with the new man. Third and fourth formers are not allowed to wear long trousers unless written permission has been requested and granted. So I'm not surprised by the reason for being called over. "Come yeurr, boy," he instructs. "Are you a turd?"

The new master is Mr Esau and he teaches geography. He's probably not been in teaching long as he does not yet have leather patches on the elbows of his tweed jacket.

School Bullies

There is a problem with bullies at my school and it's not the other boys. Not all of my teachers are bullies but a sizeable number are.

It's the first day back after the Christmas holidays of my first year at the school and we're reminded about the new Maths teacher – new to us, anyway – due to start today. He's been away in a sanatorium for a while, recovering from tuberculosis, so for all the first term we had this old bloke, Mr Todger, brought out of retirement. Old Todger must have been in his late seventies or eighties because most of the examples he used to illustrate his mathematics teaching came from the Victorian era. It was easy to get him side-tracked by asking him how much half-a-pound of butter cost when he was a boy. He used to call us silly asses (but pronounced as 'arses') and had a penchant for thumping boys in their backs with the side of his fist. For someone of his advanced years he could still pack a punch.

But he's been a pussy compared with Holy Joe, the returning invalid. As well as Maths, HJ teaches R.I. – hence the soubriquet which has been passed on to us by older boys who've been taught by him in previous years. Presumably to establish a presence with a new class, the classroom door is flung open but no-one immediately enters. There is a long, dramatic pause before a short, weedy-looking individual in the regulation black gown glares his way slowly into the room. He picks up the wooden board rubber and with eyes scanning the back row of pupils he suddenly throws it, without averting his gaze but with a force that belies his appearance, in an entirely different direction. I'm unlucky enough to be in that direction and only three feet away. I take the missile squarely in the chest. It doesn't hurt that much – at least physically. What is so alarming is the surprise, the shock, of a completely unexpected, unwarranted and unnecessary act of violence perpetrated by an adult on an eleven-year-old child.

For much of the rest of the year, this man is making my life a misery. He is responsible for the daily nausea I am experiencing. Holy Joe takes us for Geography as well as Maths and RI. That's eight bloody periods a week. There's not a single school day when I'm free of the fear of some randomly distributed brutality. And such instances are frequent and varied. A Holy Joe favourite, though, is to take firm hold of a boy's hair and slam his head repeatedly against a desk or a nearby wall. Sometimes, if you are in the room next door, you can hear this being done to boys in other classes.

I wonder if other boys in my class are as badly affected as I am. It's not something we'd readily admit to one another, although I do try to broach the subject with a nervy looking boy in my class who also confesses, albeit reluctantly, to feeling sick before a Holy Joe class. After a while, my dad begins to notice my disappearing appetite at breakfast and its reappearance by the evening meal. He's picking up that something's wrong. It takes a long time, but over a matter of weeks he manages to wheedle the source of my unhappiness out of me. I don't discover until much later that eventually Dad visits the school. It can't have been easy for someone who's experienced no secondary schooling himself, and who is somewhat in awe of the whole idea of a grammar school, to confront the Headmaster with a complaint about a member of his teaching staff. But all I know is the bullying stops – at least for a brief period. Although I personally am never again a victim of Holy Joe's sadism, some of my fellow pupils are not so fortunate.

Holy Joe no doubt feels that a return to his old ways is licensed by the fact that corporal punishment and a wider bullying ethos have both long been institutionalised within the school. An uncle has horrific tales of the cruelty he suffered there as a 'free-place scholarship' boy in the days when it was mainly a fee-paying school. It's still there and it's endemic from top to bottom. Implements of delivery include the ubiquitous 'slipper' (the rather soft-sounding name for the harder gym-shoe or pump) but also extends to subject-specific items such as bunsen-burner tubing, tee-squares and baseball bats. It's whatever comes to hand, really, and even the prefects get away with hitting you over the head with the end of a rolled-up hymn book on the way to morning assembly. The cane, though, is the special preserve of the Headmaster – and I've heard he's not particularly shy of wielding it. So, although my father's meeting with the top man has certainly helped me, any wider effects will have been severely limited.

Not the Bloody Dromedary Again

"The Dromedary by AY Campbell." Audible groans. Lewys is yet again starting to read out the poem to the rest of the form. This has been going on every day for more than a week. We rarely get beyond the title and the author because Lewys has a bad stammer. Our English teacher has taken a huge kill-or-cure gamble by entering the boy for the school poetry reading competition. The daily recitation attempts are rehearsals.

If listening to Lewys struggling with the consonants is painful for the rest of us, just think what it must be like for him. But beneath his visible embarrassment there is an implacable determination. You can see it in his eyes. No self-pity there. And the thing is, it works. Eventually the day arrives when Lewys reads the whole poem beautifully. The English master's gamble pays off. But does the end justify the means? Lewys might well agree that it does. But what if the exercise had failed? Surely there would be a strong case for a charge of child cruelty.

My own experience of a similar, but far milder, experimental therapy occurs a few years earlier. I am eight years old and in my second year at junior school. During a normal class, Mr Edwards decides it's time I learn to pronounce the *th* sound correctly. Facing me, he carefully vocalises examples and I am to copy him. I'm not sure he's aware of the technical distinction between the 'voiced' and 'unvoiced' *th* versions as we move back and forth between their different sounds, but it doesn't matter. Despite a rather exaggerated use of my tongue between the tee*th*, *th*ings seem to be going well.

"Say 'The'," he says.

"The," I say carefully but correctly.

"Say 'Think'."

"Think." Still good.

"That."

"That."

"Bath."

"Bath."

I'm really getting the hang of this – until, that is, we move up a level.

"Say 'thief'."

"Fieth," I say.

I think it's only with the spontaneous eruption of laughter that I realize the whole class has been listening in to our exchange. Because the kindly Mr Edwards has been talking to me fairly softly and while squatting beside my desk as I remain seated, I'd assumed only those pupils in my immediate vicinity would hear. Strangely enough, the outbreak of hilarity hasn't fazed me too much. Normally, I'd be mortified, but I see a straw and clutch it. Perhaps my response is being taken as intentional humour? I join in the laughter, but in an appropriately modest sort of way. I probably haven't fooled Mr Edwards, though, but that's OK. He seems pleased that I've mastered the basics and I'm pleased that I can now do something I couldn't a few minutes ago.

This Is Not Good Enough

Parents are not delighted with my first-year grammar school reports. I am somewhat gratified, however, to note the reaction of father to the Headmaster's comment at the foot of my very first report: "This is not up to the standard of work I expect of a boy in his first term. Competition is keen here." Dad thinks the last part is 'silly'.

Extracts from first-year school reports

Number in form: 29

Subject	Form position	Grade	Comments
French	22	D	Lacks concentration
Mathematics	28	D	Very poor, and apparently quite willing to remain so

Physics	28	D	Idle and untidy
English	1	B	A very pleasing result. He is working well.
History	18	D	This is not good enough.

Part 2

1960s Teenage Years

A New Delight

What is *this*? As the bus conductor walks away from the jukebox after making his selection, the opening bars hit me. Deep in the chest. The initial haunting drum, the emphatic introduction of the A-Minor chord and the first, echo-enhanced notes of the lead guitar are forcing my insides upwards. They are fluttering as if trying to escape. My arms and back are tingling. I want to stand but my legs are too weak. This is wonderful. I've not heard – or felt – anything quite like this before.

Or, at least, not in this combination, or lasting for the whole record. There is something familiar, nonetheless. Cliff Richard (my Uncle Frank calls him 'Bucketchops') and his group, The Drifters, have been performing a song called *Move It* for the past couple of years. The combination of the lead and bass guitars on that number is capable of producing some of the same physical symptoms, given the right circumstances. It's not quite to such a prolonged intensity, though, as they subside whenever the vocals come in. I'm not that keen on Mr Richard or his voice.

This new record is an instrumental but, on reflection, there is a similarity in the guitar sounds. As soon as I sense it's safe to do so, I take the few steps to the jukebox to discover who is responsible for this music of such beauty. Of course – it's The Shadows, Cliff's backing group who not long ago ditched their original name to avoid confusion with an American vocal group. And their fresh, exciting gift to the world is entitled *Apache*. I empty the pockets of my jeans and feed the box with all the sixpences and shilling pieces I have. I return to my seat and cold cup of tea in this tiny Midland Red cafe on the Newport Road and luxuriate in multiple repeats of my new-found delight.

Each time I pass the indecent ugliness of *The Top of the Grot* ballroom, under which the rubble of this charming little cafe – and no doubt its jukebox – will soon be buried, my revelatory *Apache* experience is called to mind. It is not even dulled when, decades later, I learn that (a) none of the original Drifters/Shadows actually played on the recording of *Move It*, and (b) the drum at the start of *Apache* was played by Cliff Richard.

Dr White's Biscuits

We sell everything at our shop: cakes and cigarettes, ice cream and jam-pot covers, Dinky Toys and chocolate bars many and varied. It's early days and still a novelty to help out weighing the sweets from the large glass jars with the black screw-tops. They are then transferred from scoop to paper bag which is flipped over a couple of times before handing to the customer. The first time I try this, eight ounces of pear drops are dispersed over wide areas of counter-top and floor. The second time it's humbugs. The bags are of two different sizes and hang just beneath the counter where the scales are.

Stored in the cupboard of the living room behind the shop are 45,000 four-ounce white paper bags bearing the name George Nicholson. Nicholson is not our name nor that of the previous proprietor who was here for quite some time. Apparently, the shopkeeper before him had a rather over-ambitious ordering policy when it came to small-size confectionery bags. I was rather looking forward to seeing bags containing our own name. Dad says that would be a waste and, even though the existing bags "will see us out no matter how long we're here", we should continue to use them.

High on the shelves at the very back part of the shop are some large but surprisingly lightweight boxes with *Dr. White's* printed on them. Mum's always busy in the shop but I ask her what they are. "Biscuits," she says. Unless they're for people on strict diets I'm not sure I believe her.

The Ten-Eyed Witch

We sometimes go scrumping in the RAF orchard at 16MU. It's not much fun, though, because it's too easy. Someone has cut a hole in the perimeter fencing and, once through, there's just apples everywhere. The only thing you get out of it is a bellyache from eating too many.

Much more exciting is to scrump in the garden of the big house. First, you have to climb the high brick wall in the right place. From there you can get into the branches of the old oak tree from where you can check if anyone is about before swinging down to the ground. The garden is very overgrown: lots of brambles and long grass and the tall trees by the house make the building dark and foreboding. It's still a challenge, though, to remain unseen by the woman who lives there. She's known to be capable of seeing in many directions simultaneously. Now we're older we of course no longer believe the tales of children never being seen again after being caught scrumping by the Ten-Eyed Witch, but they still add a piquancy to the whole venture.

It's not that we usually get many apples, and those we get are often wormy or rotten on the inside. It's the sense of achievement that counts – the success of getting in and out without being boiled alive in the cauldron.

Junior Ted

...or how to be a teddy boy when you're twelve years old and on a budget.

I think we're all impressed by George C. He must be at least nineteen years old and is the only proper ted in our area. We watch him as he walks down the Sandon Road, past Lotus factory, on a Saturday morning – louche, skinny-legged strides bent at the knee to emphasise the hang of the unbuttoned drape jacket, luminous pink socks, crepe-soled brothel creepers. He's rumoured to be a member of the notorious Nudie Bolton gang, but he seems quite gentle to us and we feel privileged when he acknowledges our presence with a passing nod.

What follows is my guide to approximating the look on paper-round wages and (almost) within the limits of parental tolerance.

Drape jacket
Second-hand school blazer, minus badge, two sizes too big.

Drainpipe trousers
School trousers that you've persuaded Mrs Belcher to taper narrower than your mum's instructions. An alternative is black or grey-and-black striped tapered jeans. The minimum measurement for leg bottoms is thought to be twelve inches. Any less will present problems for removal – although Woll claims 11.5 inches is feasible if you rub soap on your heels. He also advises an initial wearing in the bath so the new jeans will shrink to fit.

Beetle-crushers
A pair of thick-soled, black Curtis clodhoppers for 32/-.

Vivid shirt
Your orange or turquoise short-sleeved summer number.

Contrasting slim-jim tie
Your white tie (for orange shirt) or yellow tie (with turquoise shirt). The problem with either is the width. The solution is to knot the tie in reverse so the fat end can be tucked into the shirt between the first and second buttons, leaving only the narrow end exposed.

Brylcreemed quiff with DA at back
Instead of going to Alf's, as instructed, you get your haircut at the teds' place opposite the prison. This can be supplemented, as required, by three x one-penny shots of Brylcreem from the dispenser at the swimming baths. I've heard of a cheaper version, which involves raiding the pantry for beef dripping – but have not yet tried it, fearing it could attract dogs.

On Discovering the Flammable Property of Alcohol

One parent is occupied in the shop at the front of the house. The other has returned to the kitchen after bringing me a cup of tea. It's a cold day but there is fire burning in the grate of the living room. I'd heard that adding a dram of whiskey to tea could be warming on a day like this. No idea what a dram is, though. Quietly opening the sideboard door and carefully removing the bottle of scotch so that it doesn't clink the sides of the nearby glasses, I top up my half-empty cup. Now to try it. Horrible! I can't drink this. But what to do with it? I can't tip it down the sink – mother is in the kitchen. Solution: into the fire it goes. An immediate puff of smoke and sound accompanies the mini-explosion of ash and burning cinders onto the rug and surrounding area. Some explaining to do now, it seems.

School Satchels

A school satchel should be stout and voluminous and deserving of a good kicking around the playground to break it in. A pristine satchel is not a good look. Even worse, the smart brief-cases of the swots, the 'majors'. The leather must be scratched and its new stiffness beaten out.

Stout and voluminous, and easily capable of concealing the odd bottle of the former among the school texts, exercise books, sports kit, assorted geometrical instruments, pen nibs and *Quink* bottles, broken pencils, rubbers and the odd half-smoked Woodbine. Cider is the usual drink of choice, though – considerably cheaper due to the much lower duty levied.

Never to be donned like a rucksack, with a strap over each shoulder. A lack of symmetry is required. The correct way to wear a satchel is nonchalantly, with a long strap over one shoulder only – and definitely not across the body so that it is carried on the opposite side to the top of the strap. Uncomfortable and inconvenient perhaps, but a small price to pay for the look. If the bag is too full to secure the fastening straps, so much the better.

An Amusing Game for Two

The gate-switching game is an occasional fun diversion for two friends on dark winter evenings. It annoys residents and confuses postal workers. It's played on those streets of terraced housing with front gardens. The gate – of wrought iron or wood – will be fairly small and not too heavy. Lifting it from its hinge pins, the gate of, say, Number 47 is carried along the pavement to Number 95. There the gates are exchanged and the 95 gate is walked to Number 47 where it is installed on the vacant pins. A logistically more complex version involves a three-way swap, but either way some planning is required to ensure gate width and pin compatibility, for example.

Of course, one is rarely around to witness householder reaction to your activity so the entertainment comes from imagining it. That and the mild adrenalin rush that accompanies the risk of red-handed, in-the-act discovery of two kids taking a gate for a walk.

An Unreliable Witness

Dad is unwell. He has a stomach ulcer. He's confined to bed and a diet of steamed fish and told to avoid stress. I've been asked to walk little brother to his school before cycling the remainder of the journey to mine.

To save time, I plonk Mike on the crossbar of my bike, hoist my satchel on to my shoulders and we set off. We've ridden only a few yards, to where the road veers to the right, when the front wheel hits the kerb. Mike and I and the satchel are briefly airborne beyond the handlebars before landing in layers, and in that order, on the pavement.

Meanwhile, mother has been following our progress through the front bedroom window – with a running commentary relayed to father.

"He's carrying him on his bike. I told him not to."

"Oh my God. They've crashed."

"They're lying on the ground."

Dad springs to his bare feet and rushes to the window. Mum dashes down the road and frets while dusting us down and giving me a long telling off. A woman appears from somewhere:

"I saw it all. The big one deliberately cycled into the little one and knocked him over."

Mike is OK, barring the odd scratch or two. My head hurts a bit, the right hand is not broken just bent back, and I'm bleeding a little from somewhere; otherwise, I'm unscathed. I don't suppose Dad's road to recovery has been helped and he does spend another few weeks in bed – and gets through a lot of fish.

The School Shop

Officially, it's nothing to do with the school. It's called that because (a) it's almost next door, and (b) before and after school and at lunch-times it is always crammed with grammar-quacks (the derogatory epithet by which we are known to pupils from the secondary mods). You can buy any sweet or confectionery combination imaginable (and some that aren't) and they are cheap: four blackjacks or one giant gobstopper for a penny; a great slab of banana toffee – guaranteed to seal your jaws for hours – is only thruppence.

Despite the generous pricing, some kids have been known to blow a whole week's pocket money in one go first thing on a Monday morning. Rob, from our class, is one so inclined. Out of the corner of an eye I see him, hands clasped together in front to cradle a vast heap of assorted goodies. He nods towards a couple of final treats which a helper places on top of the precarious pile as Rob starts to push his way to the counter. Perhaps it's the claustrophobic density of the crowded shop or the excitement of the impending purchase, but Rob has one of his fits. There's the usual rising intonation of the scream accompanied by an involuntary but violent upthrust of his hands which releases a spectacular shower of chewies and fruit gums, choccie-bars and sherbet-lemons, bubble-gum and god-knows-what-else. As the manna rains down on the rest of us, the shopkeeper's facial features stretch to a sort of worried daze which I've not seen before. I'm not sure it's with concern for Rob's welfare or the likely dent in his profits, as there's a scramble to stuff pockets and satchels with the unexpected freebies.

It's not like he hasn't other strings to his income-generating bow. For the more adventurous among us, our obliging shopkeeper will happily split a pack of Woodbines to sell singly, together with a couple of matches. He's even not averse to breaking a ciggy into halves for the particularly penurious. We've heard that it's illegal to sell cigarettes to the under-sixteens, but nobody seems to bother – least of all, it seems, our teachers. Maybe that accounts for the rumour that some of them are on the payroll, perhaps receiving supplies of pipe or roll-up tobacco at preferential rates.

But if supplying cigs to boys of secondary school age is questionable, what's to be made of the shop next to the primary school which my younger brother attends? There you can buy four *Domino* cigarettes for 6d. They come in a flimsy paper pack with the cig ends poking out of the top. There have been reports in the newspapers about a possible link between smoking and lung cancer (my dad is also always harping on about it). We comfort ourselves that by the time we're old enough to get it there's bound to be a cure. So we continue to puff away.

The Accidental Arsonist

Pat calls me a bloody idiot and tells me to stop messing about. We're hanging around in the big wooden barn at the old salt works, climbing over the stacked bales of straw that are used to bed the horses. It's a pleasantly warm day and we rest for a while, reclining against the bales. Pat's parents allow – in fact encourage – him to smoke, so he always has a cigarette lighter with him. I ask to borrow it but instead of lighting a cigarette, I idly apply it to a loose strand of straw which Pat immediately stamps out. That's why he's calling me names. To tease him, I light another straw which Pat once again attempts to extinguish by the same method. But this time it results in the flame spreading to an adjacent clump, and then another and soon we're both frantically stamping all around us. Within just a few seconds, flames are reaching the roof beams and we run. I hear a panicky "You've done it this time, Roberts!" as we tumble down the steep bank and over the stream, hurdle the low fence after tearing across the short field, and cut through the allotments, pausing for breath only when we get to the main Sandon Road.

For the first time, we look behind us. A great pall of dark smoke climbs into the sky, a red furnace beneath. A few people are already noticing, shielding the sun from their eyes to get a better view. A double-decker Midland Red bus has stopped by the phone box and, with one leg keeping the door propped open, the conductor is obviously reporting the conflagration to the authorities. Pat and I, vainly attempting a nonchalance we don't feel, cross the road and retrieve my bike from the garden of my Nan's house.

With Pat on the crossbar, I pedal furiously to get away as quickly and as far as possible. As we head along Beaconside towards the Withies, we hear the bells of a fire engine in the distance. A police car races past us in the opposite direction. I'd normally expect to be pulled up for giving an illegal crossie but presumably they have bigger fish to fry at the moment.

I'm only back at home for a few minutes when the police constable calls. He wants to know where I've been and I tell him I've been at the Withies all afternoon. He asks me directly if I've been to the barn at the salt works. When I deny this, he asks why I have pieces of straw all over my jumper. I'd not noticed this before. What a giveaway. I have only tears as an answer. The policeman wants a statement from me but Dad takes charge and tells him we'll come to the station later that evening and provide a statement then.

Dad is great. Seeing that Mum is about to fly off the handle, he whisks me out of the house and drives me to the more tranquil surroundings of Severn Springs at Cannock Chase. We walk along the pathways through the ferns and silver birch trees and he listens patiently while I tell him exactly what happened. This forms the basis of my statement when we then visit the police station in town. I feel guilty about getting Pat into trouble as well and make it clear that it was my fault and that he'd done what he could to prevent it.

Unfortunately, as I discover next day, Pat has fared less well with his parents. He'd been taken into the garden by his father and had seven shades knocked out of him with a cricket bat. My guilt mounts. The fire is a bit of a talking point for a few days in our part of the town and even gets a few lines in the *Wolverhampton Express & Star*, reporting how two tons of baled straw were destroyed when a barn at Stafford Salt Works was burnt down.

Pat and I have to wait weeks and weeks before another policeman (an Inspector this time) calls at our homes (a) to inform us that neither the police nor the company that owns the salt works is intending to prosecute, and (b) to deliver a stern warning that setting fire to any other buildings in future would most certainly not be treated with equivalent leniency.

Point taken. Because of this a few months later I avoid any involvement when a couple of my mates (inadvertently, they say) set alight to 'the dwelling'. This is an abandoned, tiny, stand-alone construction by the river where we used to smoke cigarettes at school lunchtimes. Apparently, after discovering that our salon had been used as a lavatory, the offensive evidence is covered with straw and set alight. The fire brigade is called, the school contacted and the headmaster's cane applied to the miscreants' backsides.[3]

Eavesdroppers Never Hear Any Good

Clack, clack, clackety-clack. That's the Wednesday evening soundtrack as the two grandmothers gossip their way through their evening 'babysitting' session while our parents go to the pictures. I don't know how they can talk and knit – and both so intensely and incessantly – at the same time. And they knit so fast: they seem to be competing with each other to be the first to produce the next woolly jumper. We have so many of them drawer after drawer stuffed full of crew-necks, polo-necks, long-sleeved, sleeveless, cable-knit, plain… and each type in a variety of colours and patterns.

The sound of the needles drives me mad so I normally go out, but tonight my little brother is up to something interesting. For someone so young he's a wizard with electrical gadgets. He's rigged up this old tape-recorder and wired it through discreetly to the living room to pick up on the granny-talk. Most of it is boring stuff about the goings-on of neighbours and the greyness of sheets on people's washing lines. But what's that I catch, above the percussive clacking? Something about someone being a "big disappointment to them"? Mike rewinds and we listen again. Yes – it's definitely me and my parents who are being

3   With thanks to JT for filling in the details.

discussed. And all the trouble I've been getting into and the worry I've been causing.

I'm indignant and want to burst into the room to vent my anger. But then they'll know they've been wired or otherwise listened into. And that will mean more trouble – and for Mike, too. So I bite my tongue and sulk.

Pac-a-mac Hell

On holiday and Dad has a thing about us not getting wet. He insists we each have one of those embarrassing plastic pac-a-macs. Long, shiny and shapeless and supposed to fold into the size of a postage stamp, they're awful. Has he no concept of fashion?

Untidy, Lazy and Scatterbrained

Parental disappointment continues at the progress I'm failing to make at the school I dislike so much. There is also some confusion, though. For example, how did I manage to be placed thirty-fourth in Physics when there are only thirty-three pupils in the class? I'm unsure if I should be proud of this achievement.

Subject	Form position	Grade	Comments
History	31	D	Very weak
Mathematics	4	B	Works well
Physics	34	D	Poor, untidy & lazy
Biology	27	C	Scatterbrained
English	1	B	Inattention prevents him from giving his best.
Chemistry	30	D	No effort made
Handicraft	33	E	Even worse
Music	3	B	Very good

R.I.	29	E	Disgraceful performance in exam
House Master's Report: Could be a little more willing			

Little Green Fairies

'Boris Beck the stone-age wreck' is the longer version of the quasi-affectionate name he's known by. He's been teaching Mathematics to successive generations of King Edward VI pupils perhaps since the school was founded in 1550, or at least from when it moved to its current building in 1862. It's rumoured he knows all the logarithms in Frank Castle's book of common log tables off by heart.

It takes a significant proportion of lesson-time for Boris to negotiate the journey from staff room to his Number 7 form-room half-way along the upper corridor. Hands clasped behind back, shoulders hunched and head bowed, the centre-parting of his remaining strands of hair leading the way, he makes slow progress along the upper corridor. The tattered remnants of his old academic gown hang beneath the small canvas haversack containing his pipe which, judging by the smells and the wisps of smoke in his wake, is rarely fully extinguished. Occasionally he will interrupt his trek to accuse some passing innocent of some inventive misdemeanour such as eating the ceramic inkwells from his classroom.

Although old school in most ways, Boris is one of the minority of masters who do not beat pupils. We're not sure whether this is out of principle or merely a lack of energy. His methods of punishment in the classroom are more abstruse. A favourite is to require a boy to remove one shoe and sock and to sit in the sin-bin for the remainder of the lesson. The sin-bin is the green, square-topped, metal waste-paper bin in the front corner of the classroom near the door.

A more time-consuming Boris penalty for classroom naughtiness provides a welcome distraction for us all except the victim.

"Boy!" bellows Boris. To him, we are all 'boys'; he sees no need to remember pupils' names.

"Walk along the corridor, down the stairs and into the playground. You will then run as fast as you can across the playground and continue to do so across the cricket field to the pavilion. Go behind the pavilion and note what you see. You will then run back over the cricket field, across the playground and return to this room via stairs and corridor. Do you understand, boy?

"Yes, sir."

"Off you go. I'll be watching you."

Boris stands by the window and we are all also allowed to go over to that side of the room to follow events until the slightly out-of-puff boy gets back to the classroom.

"Did you see the little green fairies behind the cricket pavilion, boy?"

"Er... no sir."

"No?" exclaims Boris querulously. "Clearly, you did not observe with sufficient care. Go for another look... and *run*."

We're all back to the window as boy heads off again.

Boy returns, quite noticeably breathless by now.

"Did you see the little green fairies this time, boy?"

Distressed boy, clearly uncertain how to answer, eventually admits he still hasn't. He's dispatched for a third attempt.

"...and *run!*"

Boy is struggling to maintain pace across the playground. Boris steps out into the open corridor and shouts through the railings, "Faster, boy, *faster!*"

We all return to our seats as exhausted boy barely manages to open the door to face his inquisitor for the third time.

"Did you see them this time, boy?"

"Oh yes, sir" and, between deep gasps of air, "I've seen the little green fairies behind the cricket pavilion."

"You are *mad*, boy. There are no such things as little green fairies. Remove one shoe and one sock and sit in the sin-bin."

Paper Round

I've achieved my long-held ambition to become a paper boy and have been given the Town Round. Although, at 7/6d a week, it pays sixpence less than the other evening newspaper rounds, it's the smallest and takes the least time yet is known for its generous provision of Christmas tips. My first day is not starting off well as I've forgotten the issued canvas delivery bag. I return to my house. There's no-one home and the doors are locked. It's risky, but by climbing onto the roof of the single-glazed lean-to outhouse and then up part of the drainpipe, I manage to clamber head first through the open lavatory window. My progress is not helped by the seat being up and I narrowly avoid a self-ducking but only by my right arm making intimate contact with the U-bend instead.

The first stop is something called the Conservative Club in St Mary's Passage. It's closed at that time of the afternoon so I have to ring the bell before handing two copies of the *Express & Star* to the caretaker. On very hot days the man calls me in and gives me a shandy to drink. The room has leather chairs, dark wood panelling and smells of stale beer. I help myself to any beer mats I've not seen before to add to my collection. The lemonade in the drink is quite nice but I'm not sure about the other stuff in it. It's good for quenching a thirst, though.

Next up is the town's main police station where I hand a paper to the grumpy policeman at the high reception counter. I'm not expecting any tips from there. Occasionally I get a stale cake from the baker's shop nearby before a drop-off at the offices of the *Staffordshire Advertiser*. By now, I'm getting towards the edge of the town centre but continue to deliver to pubs, shops and other businesses as my round takes me past the prison and into Marston Road. From here there are now more deliveries to houses and I think it odd that one of them is next door to the paper shop that employs me and another is the home of a woman who works in the shop. The doors in Rowley Street open directly onto the street. One has no letter box and I'm instructed to roll up the paper, bend it in half and wedge it between doorknob and jamb. On rainy days it must be quite soggy by the time it's read in the evening.

Dirty Legs and Concussion

Aren't mothers supposed to worry that you're wearing clean underpants if you're taken into hospital? Mine seems more concerned about my dirty legs. I'm lying on a bed in Staffordshire General Infirmary and my legs are caked in mud. I keep asking her if she was there when it happened. The doctor says I have concussion and have to stay in overnight for observation.

I've been playing rugby and, as soon as school is finished, we have a football match on Bagnall's pitch. Three or four of us are cycling home together and I start to make a right turn off the main road. I'm pretty sure I glanced behind me before signalling, as we were taught to do for our cycling proficiency badge. But I must not have properly registered the motorcycle about to overtake us. I think I'm now lying in the road on my back. I feel no pain but I can't get up. Later I'm told that I was face downwards and not moving and that my friend George was in shock, still holding on to his bike and muttering "fucking hell," to himself repeatedly.

The next thing I recall is being taken into a house on the corner. On my way there I catch a glimpse of a motorcycle being pulled onto the pavement and a man in leathers sitting on the kerb with blood trickling down his face from beneath his crash helmet. I'm sitting on a sofa. What seems a long way away on the far side of the room are two young children watching television and taking no notice of me. I can't see anything to either side, it's as if those zones are curtained off. I look down at my hands and there's quite a bit of blood but they don't hurt.

I remember being slowly helped into the ambulance. I see a ramp into the back but I can't recall if I'm in a wheelchair or on foot. I don't know anything about the ride there – there's a gap in my memory – and I'm now at the hospital, asking my parents if they were there.

I'm allowed home late afternoon of the following day but advised to stay off school for the rest of the week. Apparently I'm a lucky lad. The police have told my Dad that the motorcyclist is quite an experienced rider. When realizing a collision was inevitable, he nonetheless managed to avoid a severe ninety-degree impact by turning sharply to the right so the blow to my bike was more of a glancing one. In doing so, however, he was thrown from his machine and his helmeted head made contact with a lamppost.

A day or two later, a very nice man with a bandage round his head calls at our house, concerned to know how I am. I feel embarrassed and guilty at the trouble I've caused but he and my Dad hit it off when they discover their shared enthusiasm for motorcycle scrambling.

Lots of Blood

It's something of a rite of passage, witnessing your first severed major artery. Big Phil from the year above us is angry. He's chasing another boy along the bottom corridor when he stumbles. He shoots out his left arm to steady himself and his hand goes through one of the small panes of glass in the upper part of the cloakroom door which is latched back against the wall.

With his right hand grasping the wounded wrist in a fruitless attempt to stop the blood which is pulsating in rhythmic upward spurts, Phil is hopping from one leg to the other while simultaneously yelling "Get a bloody doctor!" The crowd of curious onlookers backs off a little to allow the blood to spray safely. No-one makes any move to carry out Phil's instruction until someone dispatches JT to the Masters' staff room to summon assistance.

I know the danger that Phil is in because mother once told me about the time dad saved someone's life by applying a tourniquet. It was a time when he was still working as a sales rep. He'd called in at a small shop at some remote village in Derbyshire to find the owner bleeding to death after falling from a step ladder while replenishing her shelves. The fall had caused a glass sweet jar to smash and the artery in her lower arm had been severed in the process. Currently, though, it's taking an inordinately long time for help to reach Phil, and I'm sure his voice is getting weaker. We discover later that instead of rushing into the staff room to alert a teacher, JT had obeyed the *Do Not Enter: Knock and Wait* instruction on the door. Alacrity of response is not a characteristic you'd associate with many of our teachers.

It is only a few weeks later that I'm also close by when a second radial artery is opened. The whole school has been forced to watch the annual First Eleven versus Old Boys cricket match. Two of the bored spectators are wrestling on the grass not far from the edge of the pitch and they roll down onto the rubble from the partly demolished school air raid shelters. Again, it's a left wrist that is injured. This time, though, there is no life-and-death wait as the red stuff starts to gush forth. Just as there always seems to be on board an aircraft when needed, one of the Old Boys is a medical doctor. He sprints to the scene, the bleeding is soon under control and an ambulance called. The game is resumed, although large sections of one Old Boy's cricket whites have taken on a somewhat different hue.

Saved by Inept Carving

The drawing boards around the edge of the Handicrafts room are old and crammed with the initials and other graffiti of generations of past pupils. They are gradually being replaced in ones and twos by new ones in a much lighter shade of wood. And it's now my chance to be the first to carve his mark into the virgin surface of a brand new board. I begin with the down stroke of the 'D', using the spike of my compass. It proves neither easy nor satisfying and forming the curve will be difficult. I switch to one of the narrow chisels from the nearby bench and decide to start afresh. This is much better, both strokes of the new 'D' are soon completed and an 'R' added.

A week later, the Technical Drawing teacher is holding an inquest. No-one has admitted to the heinous act of defacing one of his precious new drawing boards so he is getting us to go through every name of the 560 pupils in this year's school book. Still no nearer: we find no-one with the initials IDR.

Thank God for my initial poor choice of carving tool.

Mud and Ciggies

In different ways we're both showing off, trying to impress a couple of girls we've just met in the park.

Woll is attempting ambitious cycling tricks in the vast concrete paddling pool, currently empty save for a few inches of thick dark mud. Until, that is, a sharp application of the rear brake separates bike and rider, the former heading off in one direction while the clothes-conscious Woll slides spectacularly and horizontally in another. As he gets to his feet we observe that one cowboy boot, an entire side of his new suit plus right cheek and hair have taken on a significantly deeper hue.

Meanwhile, I am learning to inhale. I smoke four *Park Drive* in quick succession. I start to feel unwell so decide to remove myself from company. I cycle for about two hundred yards before stopping to be sick by the gasometer – and over my wellies.

A Near-Death Experience

There are four of us idling time away at the Withies. Vaguely exploring some of the denser sections of the woods, we're temporarily out of one another's sight. I break through some undergrowth and step down onto a muddy-looking pathway – but it isn't. It's a bog into which I'm rapidly sinking and at a peculiar angle. My left foot is still above the surface, not far below my left hand which is making futile snatches at anything on the bank to hold to. I'm shouting for help only to be greeted with impolite requests to "shut up," and to "give it a rest". My right leg, arm and side of my body are being sucked down until only the shoulder and my head are still visible – or at least would be if any of my friends cared to look.

"I've fallen in a bog, you bastards."

"Oh yeah, and I'm wrestling a crocodile."

"There's a herd of wildebeests over here."

It's getting serious. I'm almost horizontal and getting lower by the second, only my left arm and head to go. There's a rustle and a movement in the bushes – and there's Woll, standing almost over me.

"Bloody hell, he has!" He kneels on the bank, grabs my arm and pulls. The other two arrive just in time to prevent Woll joining me in the quaggy stuff. Between them, the doubting Thomases manage to rescue me from what I'm convinced was certain death. I'm grateful, but maybe the buggers will believe me in future.

Comeuppance

Peanuts, the diminutive yet rotund Chemistry master, would score very poorly even in a popularity contest between the two least-liked teachers in the school. The verse beautifully etched into the woodwork of the rear bench in the chemistry lab barely does justice to the animosity felt towards the man.

Poor old 'nuts is dead and gone,
His face you'll see no more,
For what he thought was H2O
Was H2SO4.

I don't know if it's the whole world he harbours a grudge against, or just us boys up to and including the third year. After that age, he may judge they are grown too tall to pick on. But even among the younger pupils he seems to be selective. Some of us are suspicious that skin colour may be a consideration in his choice of victims. In our class, my friend Pete certainly seems to receive far more attention than any other pupil from the length of bunsen burner tubing or the long wooden rolling ruler which is used with some force as a pupil-prod.

That is, until the day Pete decides he's had enough. To delighted cheers, he interrupts the repeated poking and prodding of his person by grabbing hold of the ruler with one hand and pushing Peanuts away with the other. The surprised teacher loses balance and falls backwards, taking a couple of unoccupied wooden stools with him. Pete is standing over him, fists clenched, but allows Peanuts to get to his feet before a full-on fight ensues. The cheering gets louder but it brings teacher reinforcements. Pete, who by now is clearly gaining the upper hand, is dragged off and taken to the Head's study.

It doesn't end there. A few days later, the adversaries come across each other in the upper corridor and the fight breaks out once more. This time it's more of a wrestling match and the pair are rolling down the stone staircase. (It's interesting how the stairwell provides an echo chamber for the cheers.) Peanuts and Pete, still entwined, end up on the half-landing before once again being separated by younger members of staff.

In the meantime, there's already a feeling among the boys that the balance of power has shifted just a little and we aim to enjoy it while it lasts. I'm unsure who comes up with the idea, but the attempts to water-bomb Peanuts eventually meet with great success. Carefully hand-supported, paper bags from the sweet shop can hold water long enough to be carried from the taps in the changing rooms to the open first-floor corridor. At precisely one minute past the bell ringing for mid-morning break, Peanuts routinely exits his lab and takes the two steps down into the playground. At the signal from the boy stationed nearby, the bomb is released from between the railings above. On the first day, it falls just behind the target, and lands too far to one side the next. But on the Friday, it couldn't have worked out better: a direct hit onto the balding pate of Mr Bully, a now very wet, very angry Peanuts. But it is only H2O. We're not monsters – we wouldn't use H2SO4 (we've learnt enough chemistry to know that conveying it by hand in a paper bag would be far too risky).

For One Term Only

I'm not sure why (and can't be bothered to reflect on the reasons) but in my final term of the Removes (i.e. my third year at the school), I decide I'll show the bastards what I can do if I put my mind to the exams – as long as it doesn't take *too* much effort.

The outcome is shown in a comparison of sections from the first and third term reports.

Autumn Term			
Number in form: 32			
Overall form position and grade: 31 D			
Subject	*Form position*	*Grade*	*Comments*
English	28=	D	Disappointing. Neither work nor behaviour are of the best. *[Note to my English teacher: shouldn't this be "...**is** of the best" since neither of the nouns preceding the verb is plural?]*
History	31	E	Decidedly unsatisfactory
Biology	32	D	Poor
Art	27	C	

Religious Instruction	30	D	Idle
Mathematics	20	C/D	

Summer Term			
Number in form: 31			
Overall form position and grade: 19 C (Term) 5 (Exams)			
Subject	*Form position*	*Grade*	*Comments*
English	1	A	A very pleasing result. I hope he will maintain this standard.
History	6	C	Continued improvement
Biology	17=	C	Satisfactory
Art	17	C	Good progress
Religious Instruction	6	B	Good examination
Mathematics	5=	C	Much improved. He is now interested and works well.
House Master's Report: House Junior XI			

Fortunately or unfortunately (I can't decide which), performance in the end of year exams in the Removes is used to determine which form you are placed in for your Lower and Upper Fifth years (the two O-Level years). On the basis of my results, I'm put in LVM (Lower Five Modern) which apparently is regarded as a promotion.

But I've been there and done that – proved my point. So, once I get into the Lower Fifths, I don't see a reason to bust a gut, or even to stretch it a little, over schoolwork. There are too many other things in the world – football, girls, music being the chief ones, but not necessarily in that order. From teacher and parental perspectives, the dire consequences can be seen in the Autumn term report.

Form	LVM		
Number in form	29		
Subject	Form position	Grade	Comments
English	27=	D	His present standard is unacceptable in this form.
History	25	D	He must work hard.
Geography	27=	C	Will have to make a greater effort to keep up with the rest.
Mathematics	17/22	D	Poor
Physics	28	D	A poor result
Chemistry	19	D	Disappointing
Art	15/18	D	He must try harder.
Religious Instruction	17=	C	He has fallen away again.

Form Master's Report: He is <u>not</u> responding very well to the stiffer competition.

Head Master's Report: Disappointing so far

The comments on the reports for the remaining terms of my less-than-illustrious school career reveal more of the same. At least I have been showing some consistency. The final report is compiled after the O-Level exams have been completed and a few weeks before the results are out. Two comments (from my History and French teachers respectively) sum it up really:

"I hope he passes."

"Has made little effort and can expect appropriate results."

The Floating Cap (2)

Wearing a regulation school cap is compulsory at our school. If you pass a master or a school prefect on the way to or from school or in town during the lunch break, you must touch the peak of your cap in due deference. Failure to follow either rule is punishable with a Saturday morning detention.

So, if you have to wear one of these ridiculous hats, you might as well do it properly. And by that I mean as 'properly' as you can get away with. Not for us the horizontal peak and firm clamp-down of the swots and posh kids. The only way is as far back on the head as gravity will allow. Peak pointing skywards. If you have a good head of hair beneath it can give the cap an almost floating appearance. Sometimes from the front it can even look as though you're not wearing it at all. I was once wrongly awarded a Saturday detention for being seen without a cap until I was able to demonstrate to the teacher how I would have been wearing it. To give him his due, he rescinded the punishment, but to save face substituted it with an evening detention for bringing the school uniform into disrepute.

Just now though things are more serious. The day didn't start well. We had one of those conductors who wouldn't let you smoke on his bus if you'd only paid half-fare or were in school uniform. I decide to get off a couple of stops early and walk a back-street way into school so I can have a cigarette. It will make me late but I'll only miss Assembly and can probably sneak into school unnoticed. I take off my cap, stuffing it into my blazer pocket, and strike a match against the wall to light my *Gold Leaf* tipped. I'm about to set off again, when a two-toned Triumph Herald pulls up to the kerb next to me. I bend down, cigarette in mouth, to see who it is. The sneering face of our sadistic PE teacher looms over towards the passenger-side window. He says nothing but raises a tightly clenched fist before driving off.

I'm not summoned to the gym changing area until mid-day when I'm given a triple Saturday morning detention: one for each of the three offences I've apparently committed. This is not good news. Every Saturday morning detention triggers an interview with the Headmaster on the immediately preceding Friday. More serious or serial offending frequently earns a bonus punishment of a caning from the Head. A grim few days pass before Friday arrives. Mr Bampton appears in an unusually lighter mood and, standing on the wide rug before his desk, I somehow manage to persuade the Head that I've already learned my lesson, that three Saturday mornings are ample punishments in themselves and that therefore there really is no need for a severe thrashing as well.

With an overwhelming sense of relief, I leave the Head's study thinking I'd got away with things comparatively lightly. But I've overlooked the fact that for the past few weeks I've been on report for some previous misdemeanour. After each lesson, the subject teacher has to grade and comment on my behaviour in class. At the end of the week I then present the completed report to my parents for their perusal and signature before returning it to school on the Monday. And there it is, in clear handwriting at the foot of the card: *Smoking, Capless and Late*.

Addendum

To cap a disastrous week, next morning I'm cycling along the backs on my way to the first of my Saturday detentions, when I stop to light a cigarette – and I'm bitten by a dog. I think I must have invaded its territory. I spend the rest of the morning at hospital getting patched up and a tetanus injection, which means it'll now be even longer until I enjoy another free Saturday.

A Stupid Idea

During a chemistry lesson two boys in my class decide to ingest copper sulphate solution. They want to take the afternoon off school and have heard it's a good way of making themselves sick.

What a stupid idea. If you make yourself ill, you're not going to enjoy the afternoon. Why not just *say* you feel unwell and skive off that way? Not so dramatic perhaps, but at least you'll feel all right.

A Bad Idea

Despite its popularity, smoking in the clock tower is never a good idea:
(a) it is too close to the Headmaster's study at ground-floor level and to the masters' common room on the first floor;
(b) smoke drifting through the sometimes-unglazed slit windows is too easy a give-away to eager patrolling prefects;
(c) there being only one way in and out, there is no escape route – the basic safety requisite of the in-school smoker.

So where can the determined indulger go for a relatively risk-free puff? The bike-sheds are the traditional place, but have become clichéd and too well-known to the authorities. Ditto the toilets, (so only perhaps worth a punt in emergencies). The old air-raid shelters have now gone and the spot behind the cricket pavilion, although peaceful, is too distant for a quick drag between lessons. Since teachers and prefects often rely on smell to detect smoking dens, there's a theory that the best place would be as close as possible to existing legitimate sources of tobacco consumption. There are only two – debatably three – of these: the Head's study, the masters' room and the little place on the first floor where the school prefects gather.

I, for one, would more than hesitate to recommend any of these. I may be over-cautious, but the safest bet is always likely to be off the premises altogether. In poor weather, there are even a few cafés where managements are prepared to turn a blind eye to a badged blazer, but you will be expected to buy a cup of tea, of course.

Move Over

Instead of pushing past the rest of us, Dave D clambers over the back of his seat to the empty row behind en route to the sweet stall in the foyer. He soon returns to the dimly lit stalls with a large bag of toffees, but walks right past us. He pauses a couple of rows down, clearly unsure of the location of his seat. Then, in an apparent moment of recognition, he moves decisively behind a line of film-goers, stopping behind the one with a leg draped over the adjacent seat.

"Move over you bugger," instructs Dave, delivering a hefty clout to the back of the bloke's head with his bag of sweets. We can't make out Dave's face as the man slowly uncurls himself, gets to his feet and turns around. Dave D is quite tall for his age but it's a complete stranger, rather than Dave D's brother, who now towers above him. The conversation that follows is more entertaining than today's film at the Odeon.

The Fighting Pacifists

For two people not keen on physical combat, it's odd that Arthur J and I get into a fight. It starts with fists. I think I may have annoyed him with something I said for Arthur takes a swing that lands on the left side of my head. I immediately – and almost automatically – respond with a jab to his nose and for quite a while we alternate between periods of wild arm-swinging, often resulting in no contact, and silent sparring accompanied with mutually threatening glares. All the time we're dancing about in what we imagine to be true boxing style but what is probably more like a pair of prats being very silly. Fortunately no-one else is around.

We're both bleeding – Arthur from his nose and I have a split lip – but all this bouncing about and flailing of the arms is tiring. Our poor imitation of the pugilistic arts descends into a pallid, inelegant wrestle as we roll around the ground each attempting dominance. From time to time one of us breaks free, we get back to our feet and try to resume the fist fight. But our punches are becoming less committed, our feet flatter to the floor, legs less mobile. Energy weeps from us as we fall on each other trying to remain upright. Our grapplings continue, but they are languid, all meaning drained away; we're going through the motions.

We look at each other. How long has this been going on? Must be best part of an hour. What are we fighting about? Can't remember. Nor can I.

We call it a day. Walking down Coronation Road we agree that scrapping, rucking, a punch-up – whatever you want to call it – is over-rated and we don't understand why some of our friends seek it out as a Saturday evening leisure activity. We turn the corner into our road.

See you tomorrow.

Yeah – about ten.

Spooked

We come across it by chance really, looking for somewhere to shelter from the rain until the heavy shower passes. The door is unlocked. The place is vast and empty. There's nobody here except us. One large echoey rectangular room with windows on each of the longer sides leads to another of equal size and in between there's a kitchen with sinks and fitted ovens and shuttered serving counters to each room. At the far end is a huge stage.

The place is abandoned, anything not screwed down has gone. The electricity is not on, but the water supply is. This could be our club. Pity about the electricity, though – it would be a great place for the group to practise – and to perform.

We explore outside now the rain has stopped. Almost opposite is a two-storey house. This is also deserted save for a small crumpled pile of bedclothes in one of the upstairs rooms where there's also a turd in the corner. Next to the house is an odd-looking building: part brick, part canvas or tarpaulin. The door is locked, but it's not difficult to find a way in. There's a lot of wood stored inside – planks, poles, some doors but there are other materials, too: concrete slabs, bags of sand and cement, the odd used bucket. We go through an internal door to one side and into a windowless room with an old wooden table and a few chairs. It could be some sort of office, but on the floor is a large, partly opened bag full of cricket equipment. We could use some of that. Convincing ourselves that since everywhere else round here seems to be deserted then this stuff must no longer be wanted either, one of us picks up a bat, another takes charge of a few stumps and also slips the bails into his back pockets, a third is rummaging for a cricket ball or two.

What was that? We freeze. Must be someone there. We now hear footsteps and each of us finds somewhere to hide. No-one seems to enter but the footsteps continue. This goes on for some time. There's a gasp (it could have been mine) as I see a face over the far side and then it's gone, only to see another seconds later a few feet to the right. It too disappears.

In loud whispers:

"Did you see that?"

"What?"

"That face."

"No, but I heard something – by the wall near the bag."

And all the time, the footsteps continue – at a regular pace, but seem to be coming from the storage room behind me. But then they're joined by others, to my left. It's getting spooky. I notice I'm still clutching the cricket bat. Could I use this if I'm attacked or would I be too weakened by fear? Judging from the muted but sweary exclamations, the others must be scared, too. But none of us moves. The calves of my legs are aching from the crouched position I daren't budge from. It must be at least half an hour?

At last, Paul suggests we make a break for it. We agree but suggest we do it with a precautionary slowness, at least initially. Stiffly, we each get to our feet. Our eyes by now better adjusted to the dimly lit space around us. I notice that in two places the tarpaulin is loose, letting in the outside light at different angles when caught in the breeze. These are where I saw the faces. There's something not quite right about the footsteps as well. Emboldened and with cricket stump in hand, Paul goes back into the store room. He calls us in and points to a large, old wooden-framed clock on the adjoining wall. With shared glances to the heavens, we listen to its loud, regular tick. Outside again, we walk along the office side of the building – and past the rhythmical beat of rainwater dripping audibly from the leaking gutter.

Brylcreemed Revenge

Father is going through one of his religious phases, which he tends to do when his mental health isn't too good. He decides not only that he should be confirmed in the Church of England but that I should, too. So, every Thursday afternoon, immediately after school, I cycle up to St Mary Castle Church for my weekly indoctrination.

The class is small – four boys and two girls, all about the same age – and we sit in a line on two pews. Girls on one side of the aisle, boys on another. The vicar is OK – I know him from the church parades we attended when I was in the Cubs and Scouts. But other than an introductory talk, and one individual tutorial when we are each warned about the sinful nature of self-abuse, we see little of him. Most of the classes are taken by a younger man with thick glasses who I think we all take an instant dislike to. He's the curate, which we think is some sort of trainee priest, and he shouts at us about God's wrath if we don't do what he (not God, the curate) says. It doesn't take long to suspect that Mr Curate (I don't think we ever find out his name) is probably not destined for the intellectual wing of the Anglican church. He spends much of the first class telling the girls to stop giggling. This seems unfair as the rest of us are just as guilty, until we discover that when boys do it it's called sniggering.

During his introduction to the second class. the curate's gaze falls on one of the girls. "How dare you do that in God's house!" he explodes and races over in streaming cassock to eyeball the terrified pupil. Her eyelids close tightly to shield from the sprayed objurgations that continue inches from her face. She'd been eating a sweet.

At our school we've recently been encouraged to make a comparative analysis of the four gospels in order to spot the contradictions. It has been one of the few things to interest me there of late. Now we're being told by this ignorant apprentice cleric to take no notice of anything we're taught in school that might question biblical truth. We should be especially wary of 'science' lessons. We must *believe* and *have faith*, instead.

If I had doubts about the wisdom of attending confirmation classes – and I had many – they are now utterly and resolutely confirmed. Having reluctantly promised Dad I would see them through, I'm now seeking ways to eke some enjoyment from the remaining brainwashing sessions. An idea comes to me during the dress rehearsal for the service of confirmation itself. During the assembly-line process, we'll receive the grace of the holy spirit in pairs as the visiting Bishop places his hands on two heads while intoning a blessing. I'd come across the Bishop of Lichfield on a previous occasion and wasn't impressed. He struck me as exuding the sort of imperious authority I feel obliged to kick against (or perhaps it was just the silly clothes). So the plan hatched with my partnered confirmand is to apply a triple dose of Brylcreem to our hair immediately before the service.

It works a treat. I'm conscious of a momentary recoil of the bishop's hand when it first makes contact with my head. But the laying on procedure continues during the confirmation incantation, which I swear is delivered at a rather faster pace than those preceding. I then notice a none-too-surreptitious wipe of both hands on the ecclesiastical vestments and a distinct if brief expression of distaste as it sweeps the good bishop's face. The best thing, though, is that he must know we have planned this. One over-greased barnet could pass as innocence, but two together…?

Just a tiny prick in the pomposity of formalised religion.

Little Sam and the Big Bully

Little Sam has a lot to put up with but it doesn't stop him smiling. Except when he's really hurt. Like the time at the grassed area of the playos when he is at the far end of a string of us, linked by hands. We're moving anti-clockwise so that the boy in the centre is turning slowly but those towards the end are having to run like the clappers. Little Sam's feet are soon barely touching the ground and for a short while he is literally airborne. That is until there's a loud, sickening sound – somewhere between a thud and a slap – as Little Sam's flight is abruptly ended by the green metal post which lost its sign long ago. It all goes quiet; everything stops. Sam lies motionless on the ground and it's a minute or two before he comes round. Already there's a huge swelling above his left eye.

I don't like that Little Sam is picked on by a few of the others, no doubt because of his size. The persecution escalates until the occasion, also at the playos, when a fire is lit and a shirtless Sam is being held horizontally by his arms and feet directly over the flames. I find myself shouting at them to stop. Immediately, Sam is dropped to one side. I'm not sure who is the most surprised: Little Sam for the abrupt end to his ordeal, his two torturers that anyone should have the temerity to challenge their fun, or me that my intervention has worked. When we all see the red marks on Sam's back I think even the perpetrators realise they've gone too far this time.

Which is more than can be said for the extremely nasty person who for quite some time has been our town's most feared bully. I'd first come across him in person when I was about ten. A small group of us are on one of our exploratory visits to the castle which has been crumbling rapidly since the final resident moved out a decade ago. There we're confronted by a tough-looking bunch not previously seen in our area. Mick whispers the news that it's the notorious PD gang, named after its leader and well-known for their acts of ritual humiliation and protracted violence. We're forced to sit high up between the twin turrets with our feet dangling over the edge. If we don't each take our turn to sing a silly song or perform a crazy dance, we'll be pushed off the castle – one at a time. While this concert of conscripts is taking place, we're subject to random clouts about the head which all adds to the jollity of the gang members and to our terror.

Many years later, and in between stays at various places of juvenile correction, PD strides the streets of the town centre, barging into pedestrians and attacking them if they complain – or sometimes even if they don't. Coffee bars empty when he enters. If we spot him ahead the usual course of action is to cross over to the other side. For some reason, though, he's started to recognise me. He nods in my direction – almost conspiratorially – in some sort of acknowledgement of our acquaintanceship. I don't understand this until I discover that Little Sam and the big bully have recently teamed up.

I feel safer walking the streets these days. I'm not sure everyone I know can say the same.

Why?

In our neighbourhood three people have killed themselves recently. A lady round the corner cut her wrist in the bath.

In a house near my Nan's, a clever and serious boy a couple of years above me at our school, put damp towels round the bottom of the door and window before turning on the gas fire and not lighting it. And just a few days ago my friend found his mother with her head by the open door of the gas oven. I try to imagine what my friend is going through by thinking what I'd feel if it had been my mum, but it hurts too much. I see my friend go past on his bike today but I don't know what to say to him. I don't think he even sees me, though. His eyes seem far away. Why do people end their lives? They must be so desperate. It's very sad.

Teachers' Nicknames

Adults tell me that the names we give our teachers can be cruel because they often derive from some unfavourable or otherwise notable feature of their physical or mental make-up. But to us, it's just a laugh, and the more accurate the epithet the bigger the laugh. All the same, I suppose I can recognise that the degree of accuracy might also correlate with the depth of hurt felt by the recipient.

Some of the names refer to rather obvious attributes. *Tank* is the powerfully built ex-rugby-playing Deputy Head with the purple face; *Nash* the teacher with ultra-large teeth; the rather out-of-condition cricket lover with what will later be labelled man-boobs is, predictably, *Titsy*, while the fleshy-faced Form IVC tutor with pale eyebrows soon becomes *Piggy*. There is probably an inverse hierarchy of cruelty in that list, too.

Sometimes the derivations are not so direct as we might think. *Guffa*, for example, does not refer to the French master who talks balderdash or is prone to emitting unpleasant smells. It is a corruption of 'goofy' in deference to an amazing pair of overhanging front teeth. Mr Langdon-Davis, the Chemistry teacher with the pronounced limp, is called *Jeg*. The initials of his forenames are J.E.G.

I'm not sure what the vaguely Christopher Lee look-alike English teacher, *Drac,* would make of his nickname, but his academic gown does flow behind him in cape-like fashion as he strides chin-forward along the upper corridor. I don't imagine Mr Spencer with the bad stammer is overjoyed when he learns he's known as *Sus,* or that *Frof* is appreciated by my ex-form teacher with the tendency to produce excessive saliva when excited or exasperated. In fact, I'm disappointed to receive only 2/10 for what I thought was quite an imaginative story about a King Frotherbel III. "Too much rambling and rubbish," he'd written at the end.

The prize for the cruellest nickname, however, must go to that bestowed upon a teacher not long arrived at the school. We come across a supposedly clever sixth-former contributing to the collection of 'CTV' graffiti that is starting to appear around the school. "What's that about?" we ask. "It's about our new Latin master," he replies. "It stands for Cretin The Vile." Is there some esoteric connection with ancient Rome or Greece, we wonder among ourselves. Until we know that, we won't know how big a laugh it is. It does seem very cruel, though.

To Shop or Not to Shop

Do I shop my mates for stealing from our shop? Dad opens the main part half an hour before the post office counter to get the custom of the kids as they wait for their school bus outside. I don't know why he bothers, since I'm sure he must be making a loss as the light-fingered brigade mingle with the rest of the blazer-clad crowd that bursts through the door at 8.30am.

In the few minutes before I leave to get my bus, I help out behind the counter. Purchases are almost exclusively of a tooth-destroying nature selected from the extensive range enticingly presented before greedy eyes in the descending tiers of the main counter: Crunchie Bars and Spangles, Rolo and Wagon Wheels, Sherbet Liquorice Dips and Aero, Penguins and Fruit Gums. I watch my friend Bottle with innocent eyes scanning the choices to his right while his left hand lifts a five-bar Kit-Kat. He's about to slip it into his blazer when our eyes meet. Without blinking, he allows the chocolate to continue its pocketward journey. At the far end of the counter one of the Lancaster brothers is doing something similar with a Mars.

The answer to my question is *No*. I don't split on my mates, but I don't like them doing it – especially when they know I've seen them. I feel I'm being taken advantage of and, besides, I don't like to see my parents being ripped off. But, as often the case with matters of ethics, the rationale for the decision is not down to the one simple issue. There's the obvious issue of a clash of loyalties – to parents or to mates. Second, who am I to cast the first stone? I think of the time not long after we'd moved here. A Saturday afternoon and I'm left alone in the house. The temptation of a shop full of goodies is just too great. I pig out on sweets and chocolate and ice cream. A little while later I don't feel too good. Since then the lure of the choccy bar is much diminished and I feel no need to repeat the episode. Mind you, there has been the odd occasion of cash-flow difficulty when I've smuggled out a pack of ten Gold Leaf, chalking it up on my own mental slate.

And, of course, one further reason is always possible: plain inertia.

Ref

We have doubts about this afternoon's football match even before we kick off. With a choice of four pitches at the RAF station, we ask the referee which we'll be playing on. "The middle one," he replies.

Friday Night Explosions

Our Friday evening routine: Swimming Club at the town baths in Greengate Street; Grocott's for a bag of chips; farting competition along the Backs of Oxford Gardens on the walk home. BK is often the winner. He says he has digestive problems so that's probably an unfair advantage.

Tonight our routine is interrupted by explosions of a more dangerous sort. Everyone is evacuated from the pool, and then from the whole building, by the extremely flustered Baths Supervisor with the long nose that has a permanent drip at the end. As we exit by the main door and are being pushed down the steps to the riverside we're being treated to the most amazing firework display which seems to be coming from just across the water. We gather from the general panic and approaching fire engines, however, that perhaps the series of extremely loud bangs and the stunning random aerial trajectories of rocket-like flaming objects have not exactly been put on for our entertainment. When some start to pass us directly overhead and land not far away, we think it advisable to move so we resume the usual pattern and make the shortish walk to Grocott's. The noises become more frequent and, glancing back, we see flames lighting up the sky. We're vaguely aware of international tensions over something called the Cold War and someone suggests that maybe this is part of a Russian attack.

At the chippy we move away from the large plate glass window where we're queuing as it shakes and rattles ominously at each explosion, momentarily drowning out Chris Montez's *Let's Dance* on the radio. We're told that the source of our Friday night spectacular is not the hostile act of a foreign power but a fire at the ironmonger's store of Frederick H Burgess.

More details emerge over the weekend. The bombs were the exploding large metal gas canisters kept at the rear of the shop. There were hundreds of them. We hear of the considerable distances travelled by the flying shrapnel and the damage it's caused, including to the glass roof over the pool where we'd been swimming. The brick wall of a building beyond the baths in South Walls was holed and the *Picture House* cinema will need some repairs.

Returning to school on Monday we are not surprised, if still disappointed, to find it more or less as we'd left it on Friday. It is, after all, a few hundred yards from Burgess'. We do discover, though, that one of the canisters has gone through the roof of the first storey corridor. Unfortunately, this is considered insufficient reason for even a temporary closure.

And Another One, Please

Louis is tall, late forties or early fifties. He comes into our shop every week to draw his state benefit at the post office counter. He's a lovely, gentle man, but no-one will employ him because they say he is 'simple' and has a severe speech impediment. I feel sorry for Louis because kids tease him and some adults become impatient with his slow reactions and way of talking.

Dad is really good with him though. He counts out the money with Louis slowly and carefully but Louis always checks it again while a queue starts to form behind him. He then buys some sixpenny savings stamps – one at a time – as the queue gets longer and the odd mumble can be heard.

"One 'ixpenny 'aving 'tamp, please."

Louis passes money under the grill towards Dad. Dad tears off a stamp bearing the face of a young Princess Anne and hands it to Louis. Louis fumbles in his overcoat pocket, bringing out a crumpled savings stamp book and steadily turns over each page until he finds a vacant space. He licks the stamp and sticks it onto the page using a thumb and then, with a pronounced thump, the side of his fist.

"Another 'ixpenny 'aving 'tamp, please."

Once again, money and stamp are exchanged, stamp licked and affixed to book, confirmatory thump applied. Mumbles turn to grumbles. Louis appears oblivious to them; Dad ignores them.

"And another one, please…"

"And another…"

On this occasion, Louis notices the book is full. He pushes it across the counter to Dad and with a decisive relish says, "Now I'll cash 'em."

By now the queue is beyond the door and snaking out onto the street.

A Moment of Sublimity

I've known Dave D as far back as I can recall. He lives in one of the prison warder houses at the end of Oxford Gardens and is part of our group of kids who've grown up together in the area. Although I'm a few months older, when it comes to music, he's my mentor.

I've had a guitar since the age of eight or nine when my parents buy me an old and somewhat battered Spanish-type guitar. It has a lovely mother-of-pearl inlay around the sound-hole. But it's not until I'm twelve that I begin to learn to play. Inspired by bands like The Shadows, Dave D decides to form his own four-piece group. Keith and I are chosen because we both have guitars and Woll gets his mum to fork out for a snare drum (with stand and sticks).

It doesn't matter that the three of us can't play our instruments because Dave says he'll teach us. And he makes a brave attempt to do so. Laboriously over the next few weeks in my dad's garage we learn the basic notes and rhythms of Dave D's own arrangement of Tchaikovsky's 1812 overture – the immediately recognisable part. It's a much-adapted and rocked-up version and bit-by-bit it begins to assemble into some sort of shape.

We're still a long way from an appearance at the London Palladium when Dave D leaves to become the lead guitarist of what in time will become the top group in town. But I've been bitten and continue to practise, night after night in my room. I practise until my fingers bleed. And then I practise more. Dave D tells me that eventually the skin on my finger-ends will harden and thicken and will no longer hurt. He's right and the day arrives when I can put a cigarette out on them just as he's shown me.

I fit a tail-piece to the guitar allowing me to extend the strings past the bridge. By pressing hard on that section of the strings with the side of my right hand I can make a barely passable imitation of the changes in pitch Hank Marvin gets with the use of a tremolo arm (the crasser, if arguably more accurate, term *whammy bar* has not yet reached my part of the world). It's my right hand which bleeds now, staining the instrument's dark wood as I play the melody line of *F.B.I.*, the latest release from the Shadows.

For some time I've had my eye on this lovely-looking white guitar in the window of Harold Parkes' music shop. My parents agree to buy it for me but I won't get it until

Christmas, which is months away. They don't believe in the never-never, or hire-purchase, method of payment. Instead, they agree to pay so much a week, the item collectible on payment of the final instalment but with no interest charges. Ideally, I'd have preferred an electric guitar, but they're too expensive. So I save up the four quid needed to buy the pick-up and associated parts to convert my new gleaming acoustic model.

Problem is I also require an amplifier and speaker. So more saving-up to do. While I'm waiting for my funds to accumulate, Dave D invites me to a rehearsal session of his band. He says during their break, he'll give me "an input". I'm not entirely sure what this involves, but he tells me to bring my guitar.

A few days later I'm in St Thomas's church hall near the railway station, listening to The Vigilanties practising their numbers on the stage above me. (Yes, they do spell it like that – it's on the bass drum.) They're damned good. The sound they make fills my ears, infuses my entire body. As promised, Dave D comes over and tells me to plug my guitar into the amp on the left. He then leaves the room. The other members of the band are chatting among themselves as I climb onto the stage with my guitar and carry out Dave's instructions. After a spot of tuning-up, I begin to play the lead part of The Shadows' *Wonderful Land*. And then... Then what happens will, I just know, always remain with me. It is one of life's magical moments. Dave R, the bassist, Neil on rhythm guitar and drummer Rob are playing along with me. The Vigies are backing me! Well, three-quarters of them anyway. What can be better than this?

On reflection, I suspect that the fourth quarter has engineered today's event all along. But I never ask him as I know he'd never admit it. But, pre-arranged or not, I'm sure Dave D doesn't fully realise just how exciting – how momentous – it has been for me.

The Long and Smelly Walk

The high jump is not one of my favourite events at school sports days. I have little interest in it and even less skill. The same can be said of gymnastics. It's surprising what you're capable of when confronted with imminent danger, though.

Keith and I are walking up the steepish slope of a field next to Hopton Pools (where it's rumoured there are still submerged canons from the Civil War Battle of Hopton Heath). We reach the brow of a hill and stop. Ahead is a bull. We stare at him. He stares at us. He does not seem pleased to see us. He lowers his head, paws (shouldn't that be *hoofs*?) the ground and is making frightening noises. We glance anxiously around us. The nearest boundaries seem far away, the bull far too close. Keith and I look at each other. We both know we have to run – and in which direction.

We are neck-and-neck as we get within hedge-leaping distance. We can hear the bull behind us as we launch ourselves in synchronised forward dives over the hawthorn and barbed-wire top. My flight is completed with a beautifully executed but totally involuntary somersault, and I'm surprised to find myself unhurt.

Keith has also landed safely but one side of his face, pink shirt and jeans are now heavily coated with the khaki-green runniness of a recently planted cowpat. I try to keep to his other side on the long and smelly walk home.

To The Flicks on the B5066

Most Saturday evenings we walk down to the lower part of the Sandon Road to our local cinema. A rather splendid facade architecturally (of which we probably take little heed) hides the shabbiest, most neglected of interiors. A partly concealed side-entrance gives access to a small ticket window which allows our large group of clearly under-age pleasure-seekers to gain access to the weekly double-bill of horror or (occasionally) nudie films.

We each hand over our one-and-sixpences. The ticket seller then exits his booth only to reappear on the other side of the threadbare curtain in order tear our tickets in half (he also sells the ice-creams at the interval, if there are any in stock that week). We are now directed to the cheapest seats in the house where between us we occupy two of the long and wobbly wooden benches which make up the first half-dozen rows of the stalls.

The Sandonia is never full. It is never even half-full. Some weeks we are virtually the only customers in this one-time plush 1,200-seat theatre and cinema which first opened its doors in 1920. Perhaps this is why our sometimes-questionable behaviour is tolerated. And no-one seems to notice when, during a particularly poor film, a whole half-row bench becomes unbolted and is transported out of the nearest exit doors by a bored group of youths.

A showing of *Summer Holiday* in 1962 did attract more than the usual number of punters. It also attracted boos from the rowdy youngsters on the benches whenever Cliff Richard started to sing, but an appreciative silence for the instrumental contributions of The Shadows – all orchestrated by those of us who professed a dislike of the former but were big fans of his backing group. The following week attendance is back to normal and it comes as no surprise that within a year the cinema is closed for good. No more flicks at the San; it's rather sad. After all, we felt it was *our* flea pit.

Origin of the Majors

School: Kings Edward VI Grammar. Form LVM Lower-Fifth Modern. Class: English. Room 15.

The class is being asked by Frof Newman (the teacher) to distinguish between two very similar phrases but with different punctuations. As usual, I am not concentrating closely but I gather the distinction is something to do with a *third of a pint of milk* and a *third-pint of milk* (or some such). A posh-speaking pupil, probably called Charles (although all pupils at the school beyond one's own friendship group are addressed by the other kids, as well as by teachers, only by their surnames), raises his hand to volunteer an answer. He suggests that whereas one of the phrases "refers to a *measure* of liquid, the other..." Charles is unable to complete his explanation because it's abruptly interrupted by an extremely loud and emphatic exclamation of "*Oh mayzhaw,*" from the other side of the room. During the longish gap of startled silence which follows, I'm sure I see Frof's small rimless spectacles slip from the end of his nose in sympathetic astonishment. The eventual laughter includes neither the unamused teacher nor posh Charles, but the outburst of exaggerated echolalia from my mate JT goes unpunished. It seems Frof is too shocked to accept that it has actually occurred.[4]

A more enduring outcome of JT's wonderful interjection is in its contribution to our schoolboy vernacular. From that day, not only Charles, but all other posh kids or swots (we don't distinguish) become known as Mayzhaws (transmuted to Majors when in written form). This practice will continue long after its progenitor has

---

4   Rather like Bishop Brennan's refusal to believe that he's just been kicked up the arse by Father Ted.

emigrated with his family to Tasmania. The word, with its distinctive pronunciation, will also continue to be used on occasions among my family and friends when referring to pompous gits and Old Etonians.

Blue Leg Syndrome

It's the day after Boxing Day and it must be the coldest day of the year. Indeed, I don't think I've known a colder day, ever. The hoar frost is terrific on the trees and hedges. Everything is white and still. It's definitely not the day for the football practice I'd arranged before Christmas. The pitch is so hard a fall could easily break a leg and the pits and ridges left by a thousand boots of past matches are sharp enough to slice through flesh. It proves impossible to break the ice of the solid, entirely frozen puddles.

Only three of us and a football turn up. We are cold. I lose all feeling at the end of my fingers and then they start to ache. My feet, which never get cold, are cold. KP and I are wearing our football kits but they are covered with layers of pullover and jeans, gloves and scarves. Woll, however, arrives in his flimsy football shorts. He is shivering quite violently and between chattering teeth can only talk in short gasps. Also, I've never seen completely blue legs before.

There's a proposal that we go home. Passed unanimously.

Breaking the Ice

In the Midlands this winter is turning out to be the coldest in living memory. The temperature remains stubbornly below freezing and rivers and lakes are frozen over. This includes the River Sow, which runs through our town and by which we're on one of our routine school lunch-time ambles. JT is wearing his usual off-white raincoat but sporting a brand new pair of non-regulation brown suede Chelsea boots. The ice looks firm and thick as JT steps confidently onto the river. The rest of us are more hesitant and watch his progress from the bank. There's something about this particular stretch of water that warrants particular care. "It's fine," he tells us, and to bolster his assessment he begins to stamp about heavily. JT's last words before abruptly appearing a good two feet shorter are "It's perfectly safe."

Sometimes you can laugh so long and so much it hurts, and by the time hilarity has subsided, JT is back on land and already shivering. The colour of the lower part of his mac and the smell rising from his lower limbs and Chelsea boots confirm that directly in front of a raw sewage outlet is not the wisest of spots to test the ice.

Hanging About in the Cloakroom

I have a duffel coat but it's rare that I wear it for school. For one, I dislike the bulkiness of too many layers of clothing. Also, it can take too long to find your coat in the cloakroom at the end of the day. It's rarely in the place where you left it. For some inexplicable reason clothing frequently gets moved around. And there are often mounds of outer-garments thrown into corners or half a dozen or more hanging from the same double-peg. As almost every item will be in regulation navy or black, there is little chance of yours standing out visibly.

The continuing below-zero temperatures, exacerbated by today's strong winds, persuaded me to don my coat this morning. School finishes at 4.10 pm. It's now 4.20, I'm late for my paper round and I'm still searching for the bloody thing. I heave a large bundle off the far end of one rail, revealing one remaining coat – a navy gaberdine mac – still on the higher peg. Suspended inside – arms in the sleeves and head bowed in forlorn resignation – is a small boy. He doesn't say anything; just looks sad.

I spot my name tag on a nearby duffel coat. I grab it and leave.

Short Cuts

On days when the ground is frozen and the rugby pitches too hard for (relatively) safe play, we're sent on a cross-country run. Normally, I don't mind this: it's preferable to rugby and I like the route we take – along the Newport Road and then two loops of the fields up to the castle before returning to school. Sometimes, though, I opt to join the skivers – mainly for the thrill of finding new ways to outwit the masters on afternoon skiver-detection guard.

Teachers found that ticking off names on a register was less than successful if boys ran past in tight groups of ten or more and shouted out a few additional names (we'd take turns to do this). The application of different colour chalks to the shorts of boys as they completed the first circuit did not last long after we'd started to take our own supply with us. The determined skiver will usually continue to make one of the available short cuts undetected and thereby spend a good half-hour or so with a cigarette and a cup of tea at the Juliet.

Not all runs are enjoyable, however. I'm just over the second stile when PJ appears from the hedge and knocks me to the ground with a punch to the head. Not all the puddles and mud, imprinted with the soles of a hundred plimsolls, have frozen, and a fair amount adheres to my white T shirt and running shorts as I stagger to my feet… only to receive a second blow… and a third. There's mud and blood now. I don't understand this; he's one of my mates. But he won't tell me. He's very angry. Back in the changing rooms he's still in the mood for a fight. In the meantime I'm informed by another boy that PJ is claiming I've stolen his girlfriend. The girl had told me she had finished with him. Apparently, though, she had neglected to notify PJ of this important piece of information.

When my dad sees the split lip and other minor facial abrasions, I tell him I've been playing rugby.

Beatniks, Cowboys and a Disappointing Dad

Since father's last visit to the Headmaster (to complain about the bullying RI/Maths/Geography teacher during my first year at the school), there has been a change of man at the top. Bampton, the current Head, has been here for some time now, but this will be the first occasion Dad has had a one-to-one with him. I'm now in the lower-fifths, the fourth year of my purgatory, but not a lot has changed in this godforsaken place.

The current episode began last week when I'm sent to the Head for the repeated wearing of non-uniform items of clothing.

"What colour is that pullover beneath your blazer, boy?"

"Blue, sir."

"And what shade of blue?"

"It is light blue, sir."

"It is *bright* blue, boy."

"Yes, sir."

"What colour should it be?"

"Navy blue or grey, sir."

"And what are those abominations on the sides of your face?

"Sideboards, sir," I reply, perhaps a little too proudly.

"Are you a beatnik, boy?" Mr Bampton's voice is getting louder now and *beatnik* is pronounced in a manner reminiscent of Lady Bracknell's 'handbag'.

"No, sir."

"You will now go home to shave, and the bright blue pullover will make no further appearance in this school."

A week later, we are seeing the beginnings of the thaw after the long winter freeze. There is some minor flooding and there's a lot of slush about. In these conditions, there's an unwritten acceptance that it's OK for boys to wear wellington boots between home and school, providing they bring a pair of regulation shoes to change into. I've put into practice the first part, but neglected the second. Rarely seen as the most fashionable of footwear, I've customised my wellies by folding the tops over and down by a good few inches. Tucked inside the boots are the legs of my non-uniform, tapered, light-coloured cavalry-twill trousers. There's no light/bright blue jumper today, but I suppose the checked shirt is not strictly within bounds.

I find myself standing in the Head's Study once again. I'm facing the vast wooden desk behind which Mr B slouches with suppressed menace in his comfortable looking chair. I'm expecting another item-by-item clothing inquisition and wondering at which end he'll start. Instead, I'm invited into what, at least initially, seems a surprisingly civilised conversation. He even refers to me by name for the first time.

"Roberts, last week, as you know, I thought you were a beatnik."

"Yes, sir."

"But now I know you are not a beatnik."

"Thank you, sir."

"Now," and the way that word is stretched heralds a big change in tone here, "...now I know you are a... *cowboy!*" booms the Head, by now sitting upright in his chair the palms of both hands hitting the desk with a loud, synchronised slap.

"Thank you, sir, but on balance I think I prefer the beatnik look myself," I want to say, but don't. There's no point in a literal hiding for nothing.

But the risk is still there. Bampton is adding lots of other words, rapidly. He's standing now and I'm sure I've seen more than the odd casual glance towards his cane stash near the bookcase. Perhaps he's read my file, though, and is aware of father's former visit, because in place of a caning I'm suspended for the remainder of the week, and dismissed from the room.

I'm relieved and rather pleased with Dad's immediate reaction to my suspension. He arranges an appointment with this Bampton fellow – to give him a piece of his mind, he says. Unfortunately, things soon turn sour. Dad returns from the school, now insisting that my Headmaster is quite right. He tells me he has promised the man that henceforth I will be dressed in the proper school uniform which will also be correctly worn.

That Bampton fellow must be very persuasive. And parents can at times be a disappointment to their children.

Saturday Night at the Dance Hall

I've started going to the Rising Brook Saturday night dances. It's normally one of the town's top bands playing there: Pete and the Travellers, the Electrons or, as tonight, the Vigilanties. Although it's at the other end of town, over three miles away, there's no problem getting there. The S94 from the bottom of our road takes you most of the way. It's getting back after the buses stop running that makes it awkward. I hate leaving before the end but I can't push the parental curfew any further than half-eleven at the moment. Even so, it's 11.20 before I set foot outside the hall. I run all the way home so I'm not that late – and just about get away with it.

Promotion and Dismissal

I'm promoted to Head Boy. Not at school, of course – that would never happen in a month of Sundays – but of the evening newspaper delivery team from Percy's newsagent's. The Stafford printing shop of the Wolverhampton *Express & Star* is only a couple of hundred yards from school. Each afternoon my job is to order so many quire of newspapers to sort into the requisite number for each delivery. On the front page of the top of each pile I write the name or nickname of each delivery boy or girl to await their collection. (At least I do until an offended customer contacts Percy to ask why his evening paper always has a large-lettered *Dopey* scrawled on it.) A large quantity of papers then goes into my bag which I'm supposed to take as quickly as possible to Percy's shop for over-the-counter sales.

For four days a week that's all I have to do. I'm then free to go home while the rest of the team will still have at least an hour to go before their rounds are completed. It's not without its risks. Cycling through the main streets of the town with a few quire slung from your shoulder can be hairy at times, especially on a Friday when the paper routinely has at least forty-eight pages. One time at the traffic lights in Market Square the strap on my bag gets caught on the side of a lorry as it pulls away. My bike and I are dragged at increasing speed until, thankfully, the next set of lights are on red.

Wednesday is half-day closing. On these afternoons I sit on the step of the shop, selling the paper direct to customers. On very cold days, the boss will sometimes push a mug of tea through the front door before re-locking it.

It's not a bad job and I do it for a year or two. But there's the problem of too many school detentions. On these days the papers aren't reaching the shop until well past 5.00pm.

The boss isn't happy. I ask if I can take a day off next week. He says I can take as much time off as I want – because I'm sacked. Just as the miscreant cop in *Highway Patrol* has formally to hand in his badge, I'm obliged to surrender my canvas delivery bag before leaving the premises.

A Little Linguistic Collision

Normally I'd switch off at the annual school speech day as some pompous local dignitary drones on about his unimpressive achievements in the world of shoes or cardboard box manufacture. But this year it's a professor of something or other from Nottingham University who is talking about the uniqueness of the way people in our town speak.

I think I've always been fascinated by local and regional accents. I'm all ears, therefore, when the prof describes Stafford speech as a sort of bastardised blend of two very different influences. Just a few miles to the south are the towns of the Black Country and what you hear there is very different from north of the county with the Potteries' way of speaking. In the latter I detect elements of what can be heard in the counties of the north-west of England. Within the villages and towns of my wider family I come across accents that veer to one or the other even though its members may live only a few miles apart. But, acting as a sort of linguistic north-south boundary town, Stafford itself seems to exhibit a fusion of the two, having developed its own set of distinct speech patterns, pronunciations and intonations.

Local and regional accents are interesting – dialects even more so – and I'd hate to see them lost to some awful, characterless, homogenised way of speaking that some schools, and the BBC, seem keen on. They can lead to problems of communication, of course. I'm reminded of the time I was in Beatties department store in Wolverhampton, with mother. Her enquiry as to the whereabouts of the toy stall elicits the response: "*Men's* ties, love?"

A Little Bacon and a Little Beans

Six of us plan a camping trip. We're going to pitch a couple of tents at Seven Springs during the Whitsun week half-term holiday. But first, with the exception of the otherwise-engaged Malc, we have a trial run with an overnight stay at Beacon Hill. Pete says he knows the farmer and he won't mind if we camp in the field near the spinney at the top of the hill. He'll also probably let us have some water. So while the rest of us search for dry wood and kindling for the fire, Pete and Geoff head off in the direction of the farmhouse with the canvas bucket.

They are gone an inordinately long time. The bottle of lemonade was emptied a while ago and we're thirsty. By the time they return the fire is going really well so we ask for some water to brew the tea.

"Ah! We got sidetracked."

The bucket is presented. It contains not water but a couple of flagons of cider. There are two more in Geoff's rucksack. They've been carried all the way back from the off-licence which is quite some distance. The kettle is dispensed with and our mugs now contain something a bit stronger than tea.

I'd been intending to employ some of the camping and outdoor skills I'd learnt from my dad on our camping holidays. But by the time we get round to erecting the tents, it's dark and we're not in the best of states for tent-pitching of the highest order. We make a stab at it, and eventually we all retire for the night. I'm sharing accommodation with

Mick C while Pete, Geoff and John occupy the tent on the other side of the fire. We listen to Radio Luxembourg on the transistor radio and don't fall asleep until the small hours.

It's light when I wake. I find I'm lying on the side where Mick had been. But he's no longer here – and nor is his sleeping bag. I hear voices from the other tent.

"Where's Mick?" I ask.

"Dunno."

His rucksack is still here so we doubt he's gone home. We search among the trees first, but he's not found until something is spotted beneath the hedge at the bottom of the field. It's Mick, still in his sleeping bag and still fast asleep. The grass is wet with dew and the hill is steep, but surely he can't have slid this far during the night? Mick himself has no idea how he got there. We go back up the hill. Our tent has been pitched crossways on a rather severe slope. And last night we had concentrated on securing the main guy ropes to the neglect, it has to be said, of properly pegging the side walls. Even so...

A few weeks later, we're ready for our main trip. We set out with our tents, sleeping bags, super-size frying pan and kettle. Also, in the words of the song we know from the Lonnie Donegan version, we take a little bacon and we take a little beans. But not much else. We're not heading for New Orleans and there are no plans to fight the 'bloomin' British'. Instead, we walk the six or seven mile back-route to Seven Springs and camp right next to the springs themselves (although we only count six of them).

This solves our fresh water supply problem and also enables us to wash in the deepish pool that is formed at the head of the stream. The water is achingly cold, though, threatening hypothermia with anything more than a brief encounter – as Geoff is to discover. Fed up with the difficulties of rousing him from deep slumbers each morning, his fellow campers carry his recumbent form and casually deposit it, sleeping bag and all, into the cooling beck. Next day he's the first up.

Although we're all familiar with this part of Cannock Chase, there is always more to discover. Climbing the hills and exploring the denser parts of the woodlands, we're oblivious to the dangers of the old ventilation shafts concealed among the bracken or of the other holes and crevices that can suddenly open up in the ground weakened by a century of extensive coal mining beneath. It is not until years later that areas are fenced off and notices warn of the dangers of wandering off the designated pathways. These safety measures are put in place after a five-year-old boy disappears during a family outing to the area. A major rescue operation is mounted and the lad is eventually extricated from a trapped position way underground.

We buy additional provisions from a shop in the nearest village, but neither pub will sell us cider. That requires a further forty-minute round trudge of the two oldest-looking among us. It is probably worth it if only to take away the taste of the evening meal. We thought bringing just one large pan would simplify the cooking process. It does, but accompanied by our other brilliant idea only at the expense of edibility. Frying together, in lard, portions of every type of food from our store tent – baked beans, pineapple rings, eggs, sliced beetroot, bacon, cornflakes, and something unidentifiable from an unlabelled tin that Geoff has brought with him – we may well have produced a unique meal. But it would win no prizes on a pig farm.

The great thing about our few days of camping, though, is the freedom. The freedom to do what we want. No parents. No teachers. One of the highlights is the visit from a group

of our other friends, including Dave D who has brought a couple of acoustic guitars with him. On a warm early summer evening we're all sat around on the short Cannock Chase grass, beneath the silver birches and by the stream, singing Beatles songs, including their most recent single *From Me To You*. We're attracting quite a crowd and there is applause after each number.

Instant Regret

I discover something about myself and it's not nice.

A girl a couple of years younger than me who lives up the road has been pestering me with 'love letters'. Kids' stuff. My parents come across one of these and whenever the girl comes into our shop, they embarrass both of us by references to 'young love' and such.

Her latest, and last, letter asks for a reply to her expression of devotion to be left behind the green junction box just round the corner. Thinking I need to 'be cruel to be kind', and put a stop to all this, I tear a page from a jotter and write just two words: 'Grow Up'. I leave it where instructed and return home for lunch.

I'm not hungry and can't eat much as I imagine what she'll feel like when she retrieves the message. It will be the contrast between the elated expectation of there being a reply and the hurtful rejection of its content. I decide to retrieve the note and leave the house once more. The note has gone.

I realize that I'm the one who needs to grow up, and I vow to treat people, especially girls, with more respect from now on. I'm too embarrassed to say anything to the girl when I next see her, though, so I reckon this growing-up business will be a more difficult process than I'd thought.

A Bus-Stop Revelation

I'm sheltering from the rain in the shop doorway with the collar of my raincoat turned up, idly wondering why buses are so rare on Sundays – when it hits me. I've spent my entire childhood not so much believing in as just assuming the existence of God – some fairly distant but all-knowing, all-seeing, ultimate authority figure. But why? As far as I can tell, all the cited evidence seems flimsy or contradictory, to say the least. So, shouldn't the default position be the other way round? We assume there is no God unless there's proof to the contrary.

I immediately feel lighter, the proverbial weight lifted from the shoulders. I'm sure the weather is brightening – and the bus has arrived.

Ho! Ho! It's The Beatles

We roll into town in Dad's two-tone Ford Zephyr Zodiac with the white-walled tyres. It is late afternoon, Saturday 17th August 1963 and the start of our annual family seaside holiday. Turning from the main thoroughfare into Deganwy Avenue we are about to arrive at our hotel, which is almost directly opposite a side wall of the Llandudno Odeon on the corner.

I don't remember which of the four of us had been the first to notice, as we drove past the theatre, the large letters announcing the headline act of that evening's show. But I know immediately I have to be there. I expect a problem though. The Beatles are currently the biggest thing in British popular music. Already this year the band has had two Number Ones and their fourth and what will turn out to be their biggest-selling UK single, *She Loves You*, due to be released next Friday, has hit the half-million mark in pre-sales. The term *Beatlemania* has yet to be coined, but the phenomenon is well underway. And, with recent news reports of overnight queues of fans in sleeping bags outside ticket offices, I think it likely that the show will have sold out.

So, while the others are busy unpacking their suitcases, I'm running down the street, up the Odeon steps and through the front doors. It's only then I realise the absence of any queue. I check I've not got the wrong day. And then, with no difficulty at all, I buy two tickets for the stalls for tonight's performance. I'm going to see The Beatles – live!

Two tickets. I'd received parental instructions that I should take my eight-year-old brother with me to the show. This presents a further problem. How am I to prevent him from telling on me for smoking, which I surely will be doing during the show. Since father gave up the habit a couple of years ago, he's become vehemently anti-smoking, at least as far as his elder son is concerned. I've been in serious trouble on a few occasions already for breaking his no-cigarettes rule.

Fortunately, a solution to the second issue soon presents itself. While getting ready for the concert in the hotel room I am sharing with brother Mike, I notice a worried look on his face as he stands by the partially opened sash window. It transpires he's been trying – with little success – to erase an application of marker pen to the outside window-sill. *Ho! Ho!*, he'd written – I don't know why. So, a deal is struck. Should it come to it, we'll both plead ignorance about the jocular and well-punctuated graffiti in return for non-disclosure of any future tobacco indulgence on my part.

We are therefore both free to enjoy the show and I can puff away regardless. Back in our room later we watch as the Beatles emerge from the stage door across the road. They fight their way through the crowd of fans to their waiting transport. Still leaning out of the window, I enjoy a final crafty ciggy before turning in for the night while both of us have a last laugh at the writing on the sill. An ace start to the holiday.

(And we've both stuck to the deal since.)

A Gobful of Froth

My first taste of proper (unshandied) beer is outside of Mansfield's corner shop and off-licence. You can buy anything and everything here. All types of food, drinks and household provisions are stacked on the shelves, the counter, the floor or any available and approximately horizontal surface: oat cakes and Brasso, tins of carrots and Carnation Cream, Kiwi black or tan boot polish, two types of cheese (cheddar and Cheshire), mop and broom heads, bread – sliced and unsliced, packets of Omo and bags of Smith's crisps with the little blue wraps of salt (not a wise choice for cinema consumption, I've discovered). Among the Bramleys and Cox's Orange Pippins I find a cylinder of Ajax scouring powder that I'm supposed to use to remove the tidemark after my weekly bath. It should be next to the Airwick and the Bronco toilet rolls which we also use at home. On each sheet of Bronco is the instruction to 'tear here', which I always find amusing because the namesake TV cowboy is known for 'tearing across the Texas plain'. Every time I read it, those words of the theme song remain in my head for hours after. There's a machine for slicing bacon and ham, a deep freezer with Mivvies and frozen Jubblies and even a self-service device that dispenses Esso

Blue or Pink paraffin in return for a two-bob piece in its slot. Next to the section that sells alcoholic drinks is a separate area for all the pop bottles: dandelion and burdock, ginger beer and Tizer are my favourites, although nothing quenches a raging thirst better than a plain lemonade. (My dad disagrees with this. He says nothing beats a raging thirst more than plain water – but he did spend four years of the war in a desert where there was precious little of it.)

This evening, though, Mick M has bought a bottle of Mitchell & Butlers Cape Ale. He feels we should be moving on from cider, which is for kids, he says. We're on the pavement outside the shop and he's recounting some tale of a recent drunken escapade near the town centre. In between gulping mouthfuls of his drink, Mick is waving the bottle about as his gesticulations signal the story's climax. He offers me a swig. I put the upturned bottle to my lips but all I get is a gobful of froth – and it's horribly bitter. I decide I don't like beer and it's a good few years before I try it again.

Charlie's Friend

My form-master and geography teacher for the final two years of my schooling is Charlie Hughes. His arse is disproportionately large. The double vents of his old sports jacket allow the tweed panel in between to form a sort of horizontal protective canopy for the buttocks, or perhaps a shelf on which to store the board rubber and a couple of atlases.

Charlie's arse follows him everywhere and is affectionately referred to as his friend. As one of the few teachers at the school who do not routinely beat or otherwise ritually humiliate the boys in their charge, Charlie nonetheless suffers no nonsense from his pupils. He does, after all, have back-up.

Charlie is a keen rugby player and plays prop forward for his local club. I like to think his friend plays second row.

Shocking

Nudes of the World is the title of a genuinely shocking book being passed around the class in a pretend clandestine manner. It works a treat. The new History teacher, fresh from university, spots the activity and demands the book is brought to him. He reads out the title. "Right," he says, "Let's see what's in here," greedily attempting to open the book and receiving to him the unexpected, but to us the eagerly awaited, small electric shock. We all laugh – and, to his credit, this includes new Mr History, too.

Where Were You When...

Pat joins us beneath the gas light at the edge of the playos. His face is solemn.

"Kennedy's been assassinated."

"Bloody hell."

Party Time (With The Beatles)

A mightily displeased Aunt Nora is striding meaningfully across the road to the house that is blaring forth *Roll Over Beethoven* for the tenth time of the evening. Almost stepping over a recumbent Nick, groaning noisily on the patch of front lawn with each wave of cider-induced nausea, she marches through the open front door and fights her way through the throng. No-one tries to stop her as she pushes and pulls her way from room to room. Aunt Nora is not one to cross when her hackles are raised. She's looking for my cousin John.

But John is nowhere to be seen. She rounds on me instead as I try to look inconspicuous at the back of the room. "Just wait till your mother hears about all this," she shouts as she waves an arm in a wide arc to indicate the general backdrop of drunken debauchery. She orders the gramophone to be switched off and starts to shoo the revellers off the premises before returning to her home in disgust, but at least satisfied that her son has sensibly stayed away from the house of sin.

A few of us remain to help clear the house up a bit before Pete's parents return from their pre-Christmas works' dinner-dance. It's been a great party, though. Planned to coincide with the release of The Beatles' second LP, virtually all our mates in the neighbourhood – and quite a few from further afield – turn up with their flagons of cider, seven-pint cans of beer and even the occasional bottle of vodka. Woll has been down to Parkes' to buy a copy of the album and the evening starts with the opening track, *It Won't Be Long*, belting out from the back room.

After the first airing of Side One, Woll – who's been knocking back the contents of a Party Seven with impressive enthusiasm – flips the record over and a little unsteadily engages the needle of the pick-up arm a few bars into George Harrison's opener to Side Two. George has barely finished duetting with himself when Woll returns from the outside lav, announcing proudly that he's the first of the night to be sick. He's followed soon after, but less hygienically, by Pat who throws up over the pans and dishes in the kitchen sink.

No other music is allowed all evening as we dance and drink away the time – until the Fab Four and our fun are brought to an abrupt halt by angry aunt. As soon as she's left, there's movement from the green baize covering overhanging the edges of the dining table as a relieved-looking cousin John emerges from his place of safety, still clutching his now-empty glass.

Careers Advice

My mate informs the visiting Careers Adviser of his strongest subjects – French, German, Latin – and he'd therefore like a career where he can use such talents. "Mmm..." ponders the man, stroking his beard, "...there's not a lot of call for those round here. Have you considered the fire service?"

Bonjour Examiner

We've been warned that the oral exam part of the French O-Level will be conducted entirely in that language.

"Bonjour," says the Examiner.

"Bonjour."

So far so good.

"Asseyez-vous, s'il vous plait."

"Pardon?"

In English, it just slipped out.

"Asseyez-vous, s'il vous plait."

Er...

"Sit down, please."

It's now the Examiner's turn to slip unlawfully into English. And did I detect a sliver of impatience there? Anyway, I sit down at the edge of the long table with the examiner at the far end.

"Comment vous appelez-vous?"

I know this one. "Je m'appelle David Roberts." (With a French accent, too.)

"Quel âge avez-vous?"

With confidence: "J'ai soixante ans."

"Really?!"

It's only later I discover the reason for her amusement. And she's using English again!

"Avez-vous des frères ou des soeurs?"

"J'ai un frère."

"Quel âge a-t-il?"

I suppose I'm being given a second chance to see if I know my numbers.

"Il a neuf ans."

"Avez-vous un jardin chez vous?"

"Oui."

"Qu'est-ce que vous cultivez dans votre jardin?"

I'm guessing the Examiner is asking what I grow in my jardin. She's probably thinking we've got an idiot here – let's ask him the easy questions. Fine by me – I'll just give her a slow list of any vegetables I can think of to spin out the time:

"Les pommes."

She nods slightly.

"Les pommes de terre."

A similar response. I'm on a roll here.

"Les lettuces."

A slight raising of Examiner eyebrows.

"Les cabbages."

The eyebrow movement is more pronounced. I get the feeling things are starting to slip away. I need to be a bit more inventive:

"Les beans de coureur."

This time the eyebrows stay in place but a noticeable downturn of the eyelids suggests surprise is turning into despair. Is there something wrong with my pronunciation?

Before we reach the head-in-hands stage, she decides to switch the line of questioning:

"Avez-vous des animaux de compagnie?"

Do I have any countryside animals? What sort of question is that? Does she think I live on a farm?

The examiner interprets my confusion as a failure to understand the question. In barely concealed exasperation, she reverts once again to my native tongue:

"Do you have any pets?"

I've not the faintest what the French for goldfish is, so I'll try the easy route of lying:

"Oui. J'ai un chien."

"Comment s'appelle votre chien?"

I'm caught on the hop a bit here, so I blurt out the first name I see on the class list pinned up on the wall a little to my left):

"Brian."

We're back to the mobile eyebrows again, so I decide to get in with a deflection:

"J'ai un chat aussi."

Unfortunately, I don't get the chance to use the cat name I've just thought of. The examiner has had enough and is winding down the conversation.

It's a few weeks before the O-level results are out: French – Grade 9. (Grades 1–6 are passes. Grades 7–9 are not.)

The Floating Cap (3)

Tuesday 7 July 1964. Although in practice my final day at school was last week when I sat the concluding paper of my O-Level exams, today is officially leaving day for all us upper-fifths not planning to become sixth-formers. There is no school leaving event or uplifting speech from headmaster or chair of governors. We're supposed to return our textbooks and then slink off quietly as the utter grammar school failures we must be for falling off the academic ladder at this early stage.

Some of us have other ideas when Dodge makes one of his grand entrances. He's been at the school for only a year, never revealing much of his personal history. We suspect he's been repeating his O-Levels after not doing too well at some public school or other. Dodge announces he's just taken ownership of a brand-new Citroen van, a 17th birthday present from his parents.

So Dodge brings the vehicle through the narrow entrance by our cloistered classroom and into the playground. As many of us as possible leap into the back and, with L-plated rear doors swaying open and horn blaring, a group of demob-happy cheering boys are driven a few wild laps of honour around the perimeter. Classroom doors along the exposed corridors are flung open as inquisitive boys and concerned masters flock to admire or fume at the spectacle below them. Not even bicycles or teachers' cars are allowed in the playground. On the fourth or fifth lap – I've lost count – a figure in flowing robes and a mortar board is seen running through the headmaster's garden towards us. It's waving its arms and shouting something we can't quite make out over the noise of the engine. Dodge completes one more lap and then drives out the way he came in before stopping to let us all out – and into freedom.

It's warm and sunny, and would be irrespective of the weather on this day I've been waiting five years for. I decide to take the pleasant route home which begins with the towpath along the river. At the footbridge I carry out the ceremony I'd long promised myself. I spin my school cap into the water and watch as the symbol of schoolboy oppression drifts downstream. I feel a tremendous lightness of being, and it's exquisitely bearable.

The gloom and torment of my long days at King Edward VI grammar school fall away from my shoulders in one moment of glorious release, and I reflect on what has made it such an unhappy place for me. Later I will begin to contextualise it all within the twin themes of a brave, but not properly realised, post-war attempt to introduce educational reform, and a complete failure to tackle the deep roots of an engrained class system and the role of the so-called public schools in perpetuating it.

The more immediate recipients of my blame, however, are the teaching staff and the ethos of the school which encourages certain patterns of behaviour. Most of the teachers there are Oxbridge graduates. They tend to one of two types. There are those too damaged by their awful wartime experiences to return to their previous professions (or, if they had previously been teaching, to be as they once were). The other category consists of the younger ex-public schoolboys who fail to secure a teaching position at a major school in the private sector and come to the older type of grammar school as a poor alternative. When they get here they flap about like landed fish. Both types make very poor teachers. The first contains a high proportion apparently keen, for whatever reasons, on corporal punishment and/or are severely lacking in the required skills of pedagogy. The second lot are simply ineffectual. There are a few exceptions to and within these categories; those teachers stand out for being unusual.

But today is not just about the end of an unlamented era; it's the start of something new and exciting. The fact that I haven't the faintest what this might be makes it so much the better.

A Stink Pole Gazer

When we were younger, we used the stink pole near cousin John's house as wickets for street cricket. Otherwise these sturdy, cast-iron constructions sprouting from the pavements never engaged my attention and, until today, I can't say I noticed just how tall they are.

I'm approaching the junction of Oxford Gardens and Fonthill Road and there's a young boy, his body pressed against the pole there. His face is turned upwards staring towards the distant top as it reaches skywards. His coat, which looks a few sizes too big, is fully zipped-up but round the other side of the pole.

He appears to be trapped, but he doesn't acknowledge my presence as I pass by. He seems quite content, so I leave him be.

No Laughing Matter

Extracts from the interview for my first job after leaving school (I'd recently sat my GCE O-Level exams and the results are still some time away):

"How many O-Levels have you taken?"

"Eight."

"What was your favourite subject?"

"Economic History."

"You'll have read Trevelyan?"

"No, but I've heard of him."

"How many O-Level passes do you think you will achieve?"

"Oh, three, possibly, four."

"We normally expect our new juniors to have at least five O-Levels. Do you think that's possible?

"Yes, I think that's possible."

To my surprise I'm offered the job and instructed to start in two weeks' time. That's a bugger: I've only just finished school and have been looking forward to a long break after all the hard work I didn't put in for the exams.

I've been in the job now for four or five weeks and I'm called into the boss's office. He's seated behind his desk. I'm to remain standing.

"The O-Level results are out today. How many have you got?"

"One," followed by nervous giggle.

Boss looks up at me over his glasses. "This is no laughing matter. You'll be retaking them, of course."

There is no question mark at the end of that sentence.

"Er, yes."

"You may go."

Shaking Hands With Mr Wilson

There are some things you grow out of quite early in life – like wearing nappies or believing in Father Christmas. Other things can take longer. This is the case with my narrow understanding of the concept of freedom and its association with the Conservative Party.

I'm sixteen years old and in my first full-time job since leaving school a couple of months ago. A general election has just been called and I'm very influenced by the other half-dozen or so people in the office. To a man and woman they are all Conservative supporters it seems. I'm told that the Conservatives stand for the freedom of the individual, which is good, whereas those nasty Labour people want everyone to be the same and pay more tax.

I hear that Harold Wilson, the Labour Party leader, is due to travel by train from London to his constituency of Huyton and that as part of his election campaign, the train will be stopping for a few minutes at certain stations en route. This will allow Harold to greet local supporters. And our town's station is one of those selected. Armed with my newly found political awareness, I plan with a few friends to form a small but noisy welcoming group to jeer Mr Wilson, and we busy ourselves making suitable anti-Labour placards.

Come the day, I cycle to the railway station and buy a platform ticket. I look around for my fellow conspirators but it appears that our heckling party is composed of just one member. Deciding that a single placard would be a bit sad, I quietly leave it leaning against the waiting room wall and join the jolly crowd of red-flag waving enthusiasts as the train steams down to a halt. Somehow I find myself directly in front of the carriage door which opens to reveal a beaming Harold. Suddenly, I'm the first of our little crowd to be shaking hands with the great man – all thoughts of a heckle banished from my mind. He seems quite a nice bloke – not nasty at all.

Too Late Now

Inter-generational tension is running high in our house at present. Mum says; "Your Dad wants to know why you're so unhappy with him."

"What?" I've no idea what she's talking about.

"Why have you written this about him in your diary?"

My confusion turns to anger. "You've got no right to read my diary." I tell her to get out of my room.

I glance down at the little diary which she's left open at the page she'd been pointing at. Scrawled across the page containing half a week in March, and on which the only other entry is for Dad's birthday, is "Orrible Little Man". If my parents had only looked at other entries, they'd have seen that on each page, and in similarly large lettering, I'd written the nickname of a teacher at my old school.

I'm still angry though, so can't bring myself to point this out to them just yet. But time passes, and I never do explain.

One-Pea Sid

Pete S and I sometimes have our lunch at the staff canteen. It's quite egalitarian with the county council's senior officials eating alongside us lowly plebs, the junior clerks, and all ranks between. Some of these top bods are highly competitive. They try to outdo each other in being the fastest each day to complete *The Times* crossword.

I've never seen them check on the winner to see if it's been done properly. There's a tale about the famous Shakespearian actor John Gielgud's crossword prowess while working on a film with other well-known stars. Each lunchtime on the set it's invariably the great man who finishes the puzzle first, and often at amazing speed. One day, a young guy working there glances at Gielgud's discarded copy of *The Times*. All the blank squares have been filled in – but with letters inserted at random so that none of the answers makes any sense at all. They are not even proper words.

Occasionally, Pete and I sit at the same canteen table as a very tall, upright elderly man who normally lunches alone. He is the slowest and most precise eater I've ever seen. One tiny morsel – perhaps even a lone pea – is carefully arranged onto the fork and the ponderous and not inconsiderable journey to mouth begins. The world grinds almost to a halt. We try not to stare but it can be transfixing. Will it fall off the fork? It never does. With its content securely delivered, the cutlery is rested as a lengthy mastication follows. Then there's a reflective pause before the pattern is repeated. It is bird-like eating but at a pace that would shame a snail.

It's months later before we discover that at these times we are in the presence of someone of equal renown in his own field to Gielgud in his. And I've no reason to suspect that Sidney Francis Barnes has ever cheated at crosswords. Described recently by the much-respected cricket commentator John Arlott as "the greatest bowler that ever lived," Sidney's bowling average during his pre-First World War England Test career is one of the lowest ever achieved. Now in his ninety-third year, he is still engaged by Staffordshire County Council as an inscriber of legal documents because of his noted calligraphic skills. Pete and I discuss which of his talents might account for his longevity. The leisurely yet measured approach he takes to his consumption of food could have something to do with it.

Clapton, Beck and the Neanderthals

The back room at Rowney's is a good place to be on a Saturday afternoon. We know the bloke who works behind the record counter and he'll play the stuff we like on request. It's where we first hear the music of an exciting new group recorded live at the Marquee Club in London. Right from the opening bars of the first track of their *Five Live Yardbirds* LP– and despite a bum note from their lead guitarist (someone known as Slowhand Clapton) – we know this is something special.

It's now a year later, the Yardbirds have just had a Number One in the singles chart and Eric Clapton has left the group. His replacement, Jeff Beck, is with them for this evening's concert held in (appropriately enough) a marquee at (less appropriately) Stafford Rugby Club. The supporting act is a local group called Hipster Image whose key member, Colin Cooper, had previously formed his own Climax Jazz Band and will later enjoy international success with the Climax Blues Band. Tonight they play an impressive set and deserve the enthusiastic audience applause.

I'm at the very front and to the right as the Yardbirds take the stage, The crowd surges forward and I'm trapped in position just a few feet below and away from Jeff Beck, but even closer to one of the large speakers. I can feel the bass in my chest. I'm worried that my right ear, in particular, is hurting so much it may bleed, but I fear for the integrity of both eardrums. I can't move even if I want to – and I'm not sure I do because, despite the aural discomfort, I am exhilarated by the performance.

My elation is not shared by everyone. After each number, while Keith Relf is introducing the next, there's a growing restlessness among a section of the audience in the centre of the tent. This develops into calls for a return of the local band and, during the final number, there are boos and gesticulations of disapproval. In response, members of the group individually depart the stage with dismissive waves of their own and aggressive double V-signs from Mr Beck. I don't blame him. I share the band's contempt for that part of the audience. I'm disappointed and feel embarrassed that my town will probably be remembered as home to a bunch of unappreciative musical neanderthals.

Egg rolling at the Great Orme

My friend John A and I are having a week away at the seaside. We're booked to stay at Mrs Roberts' house – high up on Llandudno's Great Orme – which when I was a kid is where we'd often spend our family holidays. Leaving the railway station, we walk with our suitcases through the town before climbing the steep road to our lodgings. The house is in a short row of near-identical properties with terrific views over the west shore and the mountains of North Wales. We're pretty much exhausted by the time we reach the street. I realize I don't know the house number but, from memory, I hazard a guess and we knock at the door.

"Hello, is it Mrs Roberts?"

"Yes."

"We're here – David and John?

The lady is obviously not expecting guests and suggests we try Mrs Roberts at No. 5.

A similar conversation takes place at No. 5 – and then at numbers 8, 11 and 13 – each home to a Mrs Roberts – until we find the right one and are ushered in.

We'd expected that we'd be sharing a room. We'd not expected to be sharing a bed. Still, at least it's a double, and for only £5 all in we are getting dinner, bed and breakfast for the whole week. Evening meals are quite substantial, but breakfasts turn out be rather repetitive. Every morning we are each presented with a hard-boiled egg, John having failed to admit, on the first day, to his dislike – his utter detestation – of the hard-boiled egg. So, each morning, John separates the outer and inner parts of the egg, leaving the pieces of shell on his plate. He then carefully places the still intact peeled egg into his handkerchief which he puts into his jacket pocket.

After leaving the house for each day's holiday activity, we open the gate in the wall at the end of the road which takes us onto a field where sheep graze. John unravels the handkerchief and rolls its contents down the steep slope of the Orme. On the train back home at the end of the week, we wonder if anyone will come across seven peeled hard-boiled eggs and puzzle why.

Sorry About This, Geoff

Mid-1960s. I'm looking out of our front window and see Dad's car struggle to get into the driveway. He's only had the vehicle a few weeks but it's not looking in the best of health at the minute. The front of the roof is pointing upwards and there are loads of scratches and black marks. They are all over the side, too, as well as a couple of large dents. There is no windscreen. My Uncle Geoff gets out but it's a little while before Dad joins him – and that's also from the passenger side. Dad is looking sheepish as he catches sight of Mum who has now joined me by the window.

Dad says they've had a bit of a mishap. They were on their way back from Mallory Park and a front wheel must have clipped the kerb, flipping the car over sideways through 360 degrees and returning it to its rightful posture on a verge at the roadside. The speed at which they'd been travelling is not mentioned, but I can hazard a guess. Uncle reports that as they were rolling over, Dad said in an almost casual tone, "Sorry about this, Geoff."

They've been lucky. This is the first of our family cars to have fitted front seat belts. The only injury is to Dad's pride.

Soap, Sodom and a Surfeit of Shirts

John A and I start our second holiday of the summer. This one's an even lower-budget affair – a week's hitch-hiking and camping. We've tried to divide the shared equipment equally – John carrying more of the cooking equipment to balance my tent – but J is really struggling to lift his ultra-large rucksack onto his shoulders. He's well over six feet tall, but with a sleeping bag tied to the top and frying pan and kettle hanging below he's all but disappeared beneath it. I don't understand, though, why the main compartment is stuffed to bursting. What or who has he got in there?

We've no planned itinerary other than a vague ambition to reach the North Wales coast before nightfall on the first day. Four hours into our journey this is looking wildly optimistic as we eat beans on toast in the greasy spoon on the A5 just south of Cannock. We've travelled eight miles.

But we hit lucky. The lorry driver at our table says he can take us to within spitting distance of Wrexham. He lives near there and is on his way home. Over two hours later John and I find ourselves on a small housing estate in a village called Johnstown. There does not appear to be anyone around and we've no idea which way to go. Eventually we find our way to a main road and take it in turns to thumb a lift as we not so much walk as lumber through the uncut grass and other impediments at the side of the road.

Our next lift leaves us in an even more remote spot and we've been trudging along a country lane for some time. A signpost at a junction tells us we're seven miles from Ruthin. But where's Ruthin? We take the road nonetheless. With rest stops that are becoming increasingly frequent, we walk what must be at least half that distance and only two cars pass us. It's turned six o'clock now. We're knackered and hungry. When we hear a vehicle approaching from behind, John turns, drops to his knees in the middle of the road and puts his hands together as if at prayer. The Mini stops. The driver says she's delivering samples (we don't ask what of) at various places but that her final drop-off is on the outskirts of Rhyl.

The answer to the old question of how to get t(w)o W(h)ales in a mini (one in the back and one in the front) doesn't apply in our case. There's paperwork on the front passenger seat and apparently the boot is full of whatever is being delivered. It's cramped on the rear seat with the both of us plus our luggage. But we don't care; it's just so good to have all that weight transferred from shoulders to laps and to be on the move with a more precise destination in mind.

But to get there we embark on a tour of distant villages and hamlets of North Wales. Our driver looks to be in her late– to mid-twenties and she's asking us about what we're intending to do and where we are hoping to go. It's rather brave of her to give a lift to two long-haired, sweaty teenagers in scruffy army-surplus parka-type jackets. At one of her early stops, we consult the map which has been left open on the front seat and discover that close by is a place called Sodom. We wonder what it might be twinned with.

It's much later in the evening that two grateful passengers are deposited in the Rhyl suburbs. By the time we've found our way into town and made use of some rather forbidding but reasonably clean public toilets for a wash and brush-up, darkness is upon us. And we've still to find somewhere to camp. We must be half way to Abergele by the time we find a likely field and pitch our tent by torchlight.

We don't need to remind each other that we've not eaten since lunchtime. John remembers that somewhere in his backpack there should be some cheese and a couple of bags of crisps. He has to remove almost the entire contents before they're found, flattened and crumbly, towards the bottom. But I discover at least one reason for the over-full rucksack. He seems to have packed an awful lot of shirts. I count them. Fourteen! Fourteen bloody shirts!

Next morning, after trying for two hours to get a lift along the coast road, we break one of our rules and take a bus. We're heading for Llandudno where we'd holidayed a month or so ago. We re-visit the *Venezia*, the coffee bar where we'd spent some time with Cathy and Jean from Stockport. It has a good jukebox and last time here we listened to repeated playings of The Byrds' version of Dylan's *Mr Tambourine Man*. Cathy and Jean are not here this time, and Sonny and Cher have replaced The Byrds, but it's full of people of our age and a good place to hang out.

We also visit the fair. Why are some records particularly suited to the vibes of a fairground? Roy Orbison singing *Only The Lonely* is a good example but the best is Del Shannon's *Runaway*. Its swirling, almost out-of-key organ accompaniment is the perfect match for the ebb and flow of the sound as you wander between waltzers and bumper cars. For some reason, *Go Now*, a number one hit for the Moody Blues earlier in the year, is being played a lot. As is The Animals' current single *We've Got To Get Out Of This Place*. We're beginning to detect a message here. But that's not the real reason we decide to up sticks and move on after a couple of days.

Not that there are any sticks to up. And that's the issue. Unable to find a decent or cheap enough place to pitch our tent, we've now spent a second short and uncomfortable night on what amounts to little more than a park bench. But there is a roof. It's in a concrete shelter in the grounds of Happy Valley, a tiered area of gardens and entertainment on the lower slopes of the Great Orme. The gates are locked at dusk so we hide among the palms and undergrowth until the park-keeper finishes his rounds. We're then up at 5.00am to repeat the process in reverse to make our escape.

The tide is out but we make our way to the water's edge. It's there I discover that soap doesn't lather in seawater. John says I should know this from my Chemistry lessons. I tell him I had a lousy Chemistry teacher. I abandon the attempt to wash my face. It's almost three hours before the first cafe opens for breakfast. So we tread the empty streets until we're able to devour double servings of bacon and eggs. We don't know this will be the last food to pass our lips for well over twelve hours.

We reckon that Blackpool can't be that far away and should be relatively easy to get to. Not for the first time this holiday, a map would have been a useful substitute for at least one of John's shirts. A mixture of short lifts and bus rides gets us as far as Prestatyn. After a short wait, a car draws up in response to our hopeful thumbing. The middle-aged man is going to Warrington and invites us to hop in. Hopping-in is not how I'd describe the process of manoeuvring ourselves and two rucksacks (one severely overloaded) into a smallish vehicle. But we're grateful for the ride and we cover the fifty-odd mile distance in good time. Our driver gives us what seem like helpful instructions for the completion of our journey to Blackpool. You need to get yourselves onto the slip-road of the M6, he tells us, as that can take you as far as Preston and then it's just a hop, skip and a jump to your destination. What is it with this man and hopping?

But he does go out of his way to drop us off at the motorway junction somewhere outside of Warrington. So, here we are by the side of the road leading onto the M6 with, so we've just been assured, well over half our journey already behind us – and it's only just past mid-day.

Six hours later we're still there. True, we have moved up the queue. But we only have to look at the long, bleak line of hitch-hikers – in descending stages of dejection and utter misery – still ahead to convince us of the need to cut our losses. The weather has turned: a drop in temperature accompanying the rain. We are wet, cold, hungry, thirsty, tired and bored – extremely, mind-rottingly, witlessly bored. This not what I expect from a holiday.

We decide to head into town. We don't know how far it is but surely we can get a bus or even a lift?

Both prospects become decreasingly likely as we footslog the seemingly endless, straight and treeless link road that promises to lead to somewhere but is taking for ever to deliver. At last, a road with houses, lampposts and other trappings of civilisation – and a bus-stop. Time passes. A bus arrives and takes us into Warrington. Another and we're in Wigan.

Wigan bus station, past eight o'clock on a dreary wet evening. In my mind I've been re-eating my early morning bacon and eggs over and over again since we were first by the motorway. We see a nearby cafe. It's shut. But something is going on upstairs. It's a restaurant – and it's still serving. Hallelujah! We barely register the prices as we order from our table. While it's being prepared, we take advantage of the rather elegant washroom – all polished wood and tiles, and hot water. Chicken and chips, bread and butter, pot of tea. A contender for my best ever meal. And all for…? We glance at the bill. 14/6d. Look again – yes, it's *fourteen shillings and sixpence*. That's going to blast an enormous hole in our remaining budget. And we've each still got two further bus fares to pay tonight, there being no point in trying to hitch-hike in the dark.

We both fall asleep during the longish journey to Preston after which we catch the last Blackpool bus. We must be getting close to the resort as there are now street lights, and roadside buildings start to replace the fields. As the bus slows to take a sharp bend, we glimpse tents. The conductor confirms it's a camp site and we get off at the next stop.

The batteries have run down so our torch is of little help as we erect the tent with the aid of the moon and some distant perimeter lighting. The ground is damp but we unroll the groundsheet and lay it inside. I climb into my sleeping bag. There's a vague odour I can't quite place. I ask John but he's already asleep. I soon follow.

My head is just inside the tent door which is flapping in the breeze letting in the morning light. As my mind struggles with the new day, I become aware that my head is also wet. In fact my hair down one side is practically floating. The sleeping bag is cold and distinctly soggy. My top half is lying in a large puddle. John's side of the tent seems largely unaffected. The smell I noticed last night is still detectable but not top of my current concerns.

I'm up and about and trying to dry out. It looks like we've pitched our tent over some sort of ditch, or at least a significant dip in the ground. Overnight rain had entered from the front and collected on the ground sheet at its lowest point – which just happened to be under my head. We can't be bothered to re-pitch elsewhere, too much of the week has been wasted already, so we stuff something under the groundsheet at that end (John won't agree to using a few of his shirts) and we'll sleep with our heads the other end. In the meantime, the sun is out and there's a decent enough wind. So I leave my sleeping bag over the guy ropes to dry and we breeze into town.

We do some of the usual touristy things you do in Blackpool: the Big Dipper, walking the piers, almost being run over by the tram. Climbing the tower is too costly. We meet two girls from a place they call Clecky (in a Yorkshire accent) and is short for Cleckheaton which is near Bradford. They suggest going for a drink. I'm not yet a frequenter of pubs and it's the first time I'm asked at the bar if our two companions would like 'ladies' glasses'. I didn't know such things exist but apparently they don't do them in pints in any case.

One evening we go to a concert at the South Pier. Gerry and the Pacemakers, the Liverpool group who had three consecutive number one singles two years ago, top the bill. But John and I are more interested in seeing one of the supporting acts, the legendary Gene Vincent. In this country his popularity has declined somewhat in the wake of the new wave led by the Beatles. But he puts on a good show with his trademark black leathers and bad leg.

We walk around the pier a bit after the show. We're in no hurry to get back to the tent. The unfavourable tang worsens the longer we spend in there and I think I now know its source. We're about to leave when through the windows of the bar we see Gene having a drink with Gerry and his band. They're seated around a largish table. Too good an opportunity to miss, we go in. Gerry Marsden assumes John is asking for his autograph and goes to take the pen and concert programme from his hand, but John reaches across and asks for Gene's instead. They both look a little surprised, but I suspect for different reasons. Gene obliges and smiles as he returns John's things.

The week is over and we prepare to decamp. The cause of the unfortunate pong is revealed, and my suspicions confirmed. We'd placed our tent over not one but a collection of cow-pats, all having by now lost their protective crusts. We clean the underside of the groundsheet as best we can but we do get the occasional nose-twitch and sideways glance from the kind drivers who stop to pick us up on our way home.

The journey back proves so much easier – and quicker, with far fewer competing hitch-hikers. We require bus assistance only on the short final leg: from our M6 exit to the town centre. Once there, we blow our remaining resources on a sit-down lunch at Grocott's chip shop.

A Long Cold Walk on Boxing Day

Frosty Boxing Day evening and Sue and I are out for a drive. We turn into a country lane to see where it leads. It doesn't, except to a padlocked five-bar gate. I reverse to begin a three-point turn. Sue and I are still in our seats but on our backs, knees pointing upwards, car headlamps beaming at the night sky.

My vehicle may be small but there's no way that we can heave it out of the ditch. We're some distance from civilisation. It's cold and it's dark. We start to retrace our journey, this time on foot. It's not that far before we get our bearings. I remember that somewhere along this road is a lone police house. We should be able to get help there.

"Hello. Our car's in a ditch in a lane over there."

"Tough."

"Er, can I use your phone to call my father?"

"No."

It must be a mile-and-a-half before we reach a phone box.

"Dad. Can you tow us out of a ditch?"

"When?"

"Now would be good."

"No."

"But it's late on Boxing Day night…"

"Precisely."

"…and there are no buses. We're miles away from Sue's house and even farther from mine."

"Tough."

Happy Christmas.

An Uphill Struggle

Our youth club football team rarely wins. Perhaps it's something to do with the pre-match drink in the pub or the half-time cigarettes. Or maybe we're just not very good. Today our opponents are Barlaston on their notorious sloping pitch. At half-time we're feeling pretty pleased with ourselves as we're only 2–1 down. At full-time the final score is 13–1. We'd failed to take into account that for the second forty-five minutes we're playing uphill – and against the wind.

Seven Up

What's the record number of idiots to cram into a Mini? How many boy scouts can you pack into a phone box? Pete's take on this is to test the seating capacity of his 250cc motor cycle whilst it is still capable of mechanical propulsion. Starting with three of us, we are then invited, in increments of one, to add to the occupancy. The machine lowers with each addition until every available position – handlebars, petrol tank, rear light housing as well as the more conventional seating facilities – is pressed into service. We're up to seven, yet Pete is still able to kickstart the machine into life. With vision, manoeuvrability and stability all severely restricted, he also manages to coax the bike into a vaguely forward movement. Loud cheers. Admittedly, we are travelling at no great speed but it's sufficient for sparks to fly from the exhaust and rear mudguard as they drag along the tarmacked surface of the road.

It's at this point that the patrol car pulls up. After Pete identifies himself as the owner and licensed rider, the rest of us are instructed to stand aside as the officer carries out a slow examination of the vehicle and its owner. It looks as though Pete is being booked for something but there appears to be some confusion about precisely what. At least it shouldn't be for speeding.

A few days later Pete receives a summons in the post. In effect, he's accused of riding a motor cycle without a visible rear light. Some wit says Pete must be delighted with the outcome. It could have been a far more serious charge, after all.

Blasphemous Little Brother

It's a normal Saturday evening at the family house. The remains of a tea of ham rolls, celery and cake is cleared away and everyone is settling down to watch *Dixon of Dock Green* on the TV. My twelve-year-old little brother (the well-behaved son of my parents' two children) hurries into the room. He leaps backwards in a seating position to drop heavily onto the sofa into the space been the two grandmothers who had earlier been engaged in their usual knitting and sewing activities. Mike immediately springs back to an upright position with an almighty shriek of "Jesus fucking Christ!" Dixon is temporarily ignored as we all turn in shock, astonishment or curiosity (depending on the generation) to discover the large pair of upturned scissors lodged between the sofa seats – and pointing in a vertically frightening direction.[5]

"How did those get there?" did I hear from some part of the room?

Rocking The Boat

Each year some kids across our county get to go on a schools' cruise organised by the local education authority that I work for. In return for a little routine on-board admin work, a free place on the ship is offered to a younger member of staff. The opportunity will normally go to someone recently successful in an early stage of their local government exams. It's seen as a staged reward-cum-incentive during the gruelling five or more years of part-time study towards their professional qualification.

5   I've wondered since if this episode coincided with the start – or end – of my brother's religious phase.

This year, there's two of us in that position. Who will the Deputy Chief Education Officer choose to be the lucky cruiser: the long-haired, trouble-making, active trades unionist or the clean-cut, conventionally dressed young man who doesn't rock the boat?

In the end, I'm rather pleased I'm not invited. The *MS Devonia* is an old troop-ship built in 1939 and now, with the scrapyard beckoning, on its last sea-legs. Unfortunately, the vast majority of those aboard do not get the chance to develop sea-legs of their own. The *Devonia* is not the most stable of craft in the first place, and this year's cruise is bedevilled by day after day of rough seas from a series of severe storms. It's reported that over ninety per cent of the passengers, and even half of the crew, are sea-sick. No boat-rocking required from anyone, it seems.

An Ambivalent Relationship

The relationship between my dad and his mother-in-law is a complex one. There's genuine affection on both sides, but there's also a degree or two of mutual suspicion. To my knowledge I've never witnessed overt conflict or hostility. There are, though, occasional hints of some deep-seated resentment, perhaps relating to episodes in the immediate post-war years when Mum and Dad were living in my nan's house.

So, instead of argument, there's the mild teasing and the practical jokes. The latter, though, is a one-sided affair – my dad making all the running. There are the old favourites: tying her apron strings to the rungs of the chair, or the weekly pretence of barely being able to lift the slice of nan's home-baked cake.

Yesterday's one-off, though, is my current favourite. While she puts on her coat at the end of her visit, I catch dad slipping a little something into nan's handbag before her bus journey home. Today, my broadly grinning father is getting his ear-chewed off by an irate mother-in-law on the other end of the phone. Apparently, my proudly teetotal grandmother is mortified by what she and the bus conductor see as she prepares to pay her fare. She opens her bag to reach for her purse, and there – in open view of both – is the almost empty half-bottle of Johnnie Walker.

Last Words

Sometimes I wish I'd kept my mouth shut. I'm unhappy with the way Skelly has played today and I tell him so. Our team has just been defeated – again – and I don't think he's been taking the game seriously enough.

A few hours later Skelly is dead, killed when his car leaves the road near Milford.

Beware of Art Students

Mother asks, "What does your new girlfriend do?"

"She's a student at the Art College."

"You want to be careful you don't catch VD."

"!"

Mods, Rockers and Defenestration

It promises to be an eventful week when the hefty looking man lands on the pavement close to our table. He seems a little surprised, but otherwise unharmed, as he gets to his feet. Brushing the shards of glass from his shirt and jeans, he walks slowly away. After the almighty cheer from within that accompanies the unorthodox ejection through the large unopened window, normal Saturday evening pub activity resumes.

Fred and I are having a drink near the sea front and not far from the Britannia Pier at the end of our first day in Great Yarmouth. Neither of us has ever visited anywhere on the east coast before. Living in the West Midlands, the coasts of north Wales and the north-west are more accessible. But for a change, we'd stuck a pin in my motoring atlas and this brash and breezy Norfolk resort turns out the lucky recipient of our holiday spending money.

Not that we're flush with the stuff, though. Fred's funds have seriously depleted of late with his purchase of a brand new *Ludwig* drum kit. In fact, it's only by receiving a first instalment on the sale of his old drums that he's able to afford a holiday at all. And my reserves have taken a hit by paying the first instalment on a second-hand set of drums. Before leaving home for our trip eastwards, I'd stashed the base drum, snare, tom-toms, hi-hat, cymbals and stool in the loft. Anticipating parental opposition, it's important I pick the right time to announce my acquisition.

We travel the two hundred miles to Yarmouth overnight, joining the crawling traffic a mile or two before the town's only river crossing at about nine o'clock this morning. Our arrival is not greeted with open arms. We're refused admission to every campsite we try, either because they're 'full' or because Fred and I are 'not a married couple'. Strange place.

By the time we find a spot to pitch our tent, just outside Yarmouth near a stock-car track and stadium, the temperature has rocketed. Even though we've had all the car's windows open, it's still hot and sticky. We're also tired and hungry. The field is so over-stuffed with tents that it's impossible to peg all the sides down properly. The site is more like a makeshift refugee camp than a pleasant vacation retreat; the amenities non-existent other than a single, smelly and woefully inadequate toilet block with one outside tap. We vow to spend as little time there as possible, returning to the site only at night times to trip over the vast web of guy ropes on the way back to the tent.

We feel better after driving into town to enjoy a long-overdue but truly satisfying meal of sausage, egg, chips, bread and marge and a cup of tea – and all for 3/6d. We're so impressed with the quality and the price that we return to the same sea-front cafe every day for our main meal. (In fact, given the need to keep costs down, it's normally our only meal.)

We're even more tired now so on this very hot, beautifully clear-blue-sky afternoon we remove our shirts and lie down on the burning sands. I switch on the radio to listen to the commentary of England's World Cup quarter-final match. Unfortunately, we don't hear what will become the memorable incident of the Argentinian captain's refusal to leave the field after an arguably unjust dismissal by the ref. We also fail to catch Geoff Hurst scoring the only goal of the game – enough to propel England into the semi-finals and on their way to victory in the final one week from today.

In fact we miss all but the first few minutes, and it's early evening when we wake. Fred's back and shoulders are already all red and he says my face has caught the sun, too. It's with glowing skin that we take our freshly poured pints from the bar and grab an outside table as soon as it's vacated. We're barely half way through our drinks when the defenestration occurs. Fearing the deposit of stray fragments we leave the remainder of our beers and move on. There are too many other windows close by and, in any case, the beer is pretty awful there.

We walk past the candy-floss stalls and amusement arcades and through the holiday crowds of a busy Marine Parade and find a likely pub nearer the other pier. The atmosphere of this place is less tense – Fred is beginning to feel the effects of his over-exposure to the sun – but the beer is no better. So we stick to shorts whilst through the large window we watch the world outside go by. The world in this stretch of the sea-front contains more leather jackets and motorbikes in contrast to the Lambrettas and parkas at the other end.

This becomes far more apparent the following afternoon when we're about to enter the Pleasure Beach. A scooterised mod has strayed into enemy territory. We watch as he's forced to slow down approaching a gathering chicane of leather and sleeveless denim in the road ahead. As he attempts to negotiate his way through the narrowing gap, the unfortunate rider is separated from his machine – surprisingly quite gently – by a lifting hand from either side. As the scooter is left to wobble on to its grating fall, the mod disappears into a crush of spirited rockers. Fred and I continue our way through the entrance to investigate the other entertainment on offer. We're particularly taken with the go-karts. Even though it's five bob a throw we'll return to them frequently over the next few days, despite a badly peeling Fred continuing to display signs of heat exhaustion.

In the days leading up to our holiday, there'd been the occasional rasping sound from my car's exhaust. I'd traced it to a small hole in the rusting silencer but chose to ignore it. By mid-week the long Friday night journey and the daily drives in and out of Yarmouth had expanded the hole considerably. The roar as we make our way along Marine Parade is now turning heads. I think they expect to see a powerful hot-rod lamming it along the front and are disappointed when an eleven-year-old 848cc Austin A30 pootles past. The unwanted attention we're attracting includes that of the town police who advise me to get it seen to. I can't afford it, so we'd best keep a lower profile. A change of scenery would be good in any case.

So, on a blisteringly hot day we park up – to the strains of The Loving Spoonful's *Summer In The City* – somewhere in the nearby port of Lowestoft. *"Back of my neck getting dirty and gritty…"* that clumsy second line of the song is greeted with a rueful nod by Fred. We open our doors, step outside and sniff the air. We'd heard that this place still hosts an active fishing fleet with associated storage and distribution facilities, but this is ridiculous. The place stinks! We take one look at each other over the top of the car, get back in and return to Yarmouth. Hot days and populations of landed fish are not a good mix.

The car is noisier than ever so we park quite a distance from the sea front to avoid further discussion with the local constabulary. Through open doors and windows, *Sunny Afternoon*, last week's chart-topper by The Kinks, is playing on jukeboxes and tinny radios as we stroll our way through the streets and to the beach. Fred is still feeling a bit under the weather so we take it easy for the rest of the day. We sit around on and near the beach, lazily explore a couple of amusement arcades and eat chips from the market in the town centre. When we head off in the general direction of the car, we can't find it. It takes almost an hour-and-a-half – trudging what must be every street in Yarmouth – before we come across it.

We'd intended to stay the week, but by Thursday the weather has turned, Fred is still not a hundred per cent and he says he's missing his new girlfriend. Our main reason for leaving prematurely, though, is we're broke. Go-karts and pub whisky don't come cheap. We roll up the tent, load up the car and make an earlyish start on the noisy journey home. This week's Number One is Georgie Fame's *Get Away* which is played a lot on the way back, fading in and out with the faltering Radio Caroline reception.

The trouble begins just past Swaffham. The engine is rebelling against the instructions of the accelerator pedal. The vehicle stutters to a stop and refuses to re-start. This has happened a couple of times in the past and I know what to do. I have to unbolt the carburettor and clean the jets. Dad reckons they must get silted up from muck in the petrol tank. The process takes longer than it should because we have to unload everything from the boot to find my spanners.

The same thing happens again before Peterborough – and near Leicester – and, really annoyingly, just four miles from Fred's house. And that's without detailing the worsening clamour from the exhaust system, the series of traffic jams – oh, and the puncture. It's early evening by the time I reach home. And I'm in no mood to be confronted by two parents adamant in their refusal to allow drums on the premises. It must be years since either of them has climbed into the attic. Why *this* week?

I Would Walk Fifty Miles... But No More

It's not the wisest of actions to preface the fifty-mile walk with a visit to the pub. And no doubt it's equally silly to survive the following sixteen hours on a diet of sugar tablets and a shared small bottle of brandy (supplemented by a single rock cake at the first 'rest' station).

But it is in good spirits that at 10.00 o'clock on a clear evening a small group of us joins the massed band of starters at Milford Common for the beginning of the charity walk. Without much consideration, we'd decided to put our names down for the event – more for a laugh than anything else. As we glanced at the sketch map of the planned route linking villages in a wide circle around the town, I don't think any of us thought seriously about finishing the course. But it would be interesting to see how far we could or would get.

A few miles past the first scheduled stop, Woll and I find we've got into the stride of things and we're quite enjoying it. Perhaps it's the brandy, which we've now finished off. My feet are holding up OK: no blisters as yet. Following advice to harden the skin in preparation for the event, over the past three or four days I've been making regular applications of surgical spirit. Admittedly we'd been told to begin this routine at least a fortnight in advance, but I was late in getting round to it. Still, I'm thinking that the first rest station, after just twelve miles, was too early in the walk.

These stations are places to grab a cup of tea and some water and, if needed, to get your blisters sliced. There are just two planned for the entire route. The other is at thirty miles, and then there's nothing over the long remaining stretch when you'd have thought anyone still in the walk would most welcome it.

It's a long way before the second break when the first twinges start. It's my right foot that's the first to complain, but the other is soon in sympathy. I'd heard it's not a good idea to wear new boots that have not been broken in. So a few days ago a workmate loaned me a stout pair which he said had stood him in good stead for years. They're my size and seemed quite comfortable when I tried them on. But of course they're moulded to his feet, not mine, and I'm sensing resistance. Woll is suffering, too, but his problem is not borrowed footgear. The thin soles of his everyday shoes are providing insufficient protection for trekking on hard roadways. I suppose the Cuban heels are not helping either. But we plod on as the blisters accumulate, get bigger and, I swear, develop blisters of their own. We barely notice the unfolding dawn as we console each other that in a few more miles, some kind St. John's volunteer will slit them for us.

And this does indeed provide some relief. After a half-hour break for the medical attention and a cup of tea, it's difficult getting into the boots again and even harder to force ourselves to return to the walk. But back on the road, we're more or less hobble-free for a few miles. We know the worst is yet to come, though, so we're disappointed rather than surprised when fresh crops of blisters begin to sprout.

It's worse walking in daylight, especially when you see long stretches of hardly diminishing road laid out in front. At no stage has either of us raised the question of quitting or of completing but by now we both know the answer. Conversation is sparse, our progression trance-like and somehow we get through the long hours of the morning. We come across a small group of fellow walkers I recognise from the start. In the warm sunshine, they're sprawled in various attitudes on the inviting grass verge at a road junction. Two have their eyes closed, motionless. We gratefully accept the offer of swigs of orange squash which we take still standing. It is so tempting to lie or even sit here a while – to re-charge for the final assault. But that could prove fatal for mission completion. I see now why there is no rest station over the last twenty miles of the route. If we paused now, I doubt I could get up again for a week. The finishing line is no more than two miles away. It would be foolish not to press on immediately. Maybe just for one minute…

Woll is shaking my shoulder, urging me up. How long have I been out? Two minutes at most, he says, pulling me up now. Unable to rouse their two slumbering chums, the orange squash purveyors are already up and away. Woll and I follow in what is now the longest three-quarters of an hour of my life. We're almost within spitting distance of Milford when I straighten out a bit from my huddled limp as people begin clapping us from their front gardens. I hadn't expected that. A bit embarrassing really.

And then it's over. There are smiles, congratulations and further handclaps from the walk's organizers and helpers as we're guided to the makeshift canteen in the car park of the Barley Mow where we're given tea and buns. After crossing the road, we fall onto the grass. I remove my boots and watch some of the remaining walkers cross the line. One lad collapses, and it takes the St John's Ambulance squad some time to bring him round.

I'm too tired to sleep but it's good enough just sitting here half-dazed for the time being. Some of the helpers are providing lifts home. When my turn comes I'm relieved to accept the offer as I find my feet are now too swollen to accept the boots. To save the van driver turning off the main road, I show him where I'd like to be dropped off. My home is very close but those remaining three hundred yards in stockinged feet are the most painful of the whole weekend.

It's a struggle getting into work next day. I'm an hour late as I open the door into the accounts office – a fair proportion of that time having been spent gingerly climbing the two flights of stone stairs. But instead of the expected bollocking, I'm greeted to a standing ovation from my fellow wage-slaves and the boss. Three rounds of applause within the last twenty-four hours. I'm not used to this.

Would I do it again?

No.

Beer and Smog

To a dance hall in Wellington where The Vigilanties play a good first half set. During the break, Anne and I nip across the road for a drink. Anne, wisely as it turns out, has a vodka. I buy a pint of bitter. It's cloudy – best leave it to settle. I look around. All the men (and it is only men, Anne is the sole female in there) are drinking the dark mild. I think little of it: it's obviously a solidly working-class pub and we are bordering the Black Country.

My beer is still looking a little... stodgy, and there are bits in it, lots of them. A sip would probably have been better than a swig, as a tester. That is vile. I've not tasted anything like it before. I have my doubts but maybe it's an acquired taste, a peculiarity of the local brew. I'll give it another try. Still awful but perhaps marginally better than the first pull. I judge it's not the sort of place for a stranger to complain and demand a replacement. Even leaving a near-full glass on the table could make for an awkward exit.

Besides, I've paid 1/7d for this sludge so I won't let it beat me. I don't think I can bare to make repeated small mouthfuls of the stuff and in any case, we need to get back for the rest of the dance. There's only one way to do this. I pick up the glass, close my eyes and down it in one. Like the old spittoon joke, it was probably all in one piece anyway.

I do miss the first few numbers of the Vigies' second half performance. I'm sitting on a low wall outside the building, waiting for the acute nausea to abate to a safe level and cursing my stupidity for not ordering the mild. It would have been a penny cheaper, too. Feeling somewhat better I stand up, vaguely aware of a descending mist, and return to the dance.

The mist has thickened to a fog by the time we leave and it takes a few minutes to find the car. If it persists it'll be a long drive home. It does more than maintain itself, however. A few miles into the journey we're at snail pace – and completely lost. It's now a proper pea-souper. You feel you could cut through the engulfing yellow blanket with a knife. And you can taste it. On the grounds of both flavour and density, it's a close run thing this evening between the smog and the beer.

Eventually there's a red light directly in front of us – two in fact – and they're moving, just about. This is good: we'll just follow the tail lights of this vehicle in front so should end up at least somewhere. We're very close behind but there's little chance of a bump as we're crawling along, rarely out of first gear. This goes on for the best part of an hour when the crawl becomes a halt. Traffic lights? Junction? I wait. Anne has been asleep for a while, no doubt anaesthetised by the soft music on the only station we can get on her radio, and I'm now nodding, too.

It's cold when I wake. I'm just noticing that the fog has lifted when I'm startled by a rap on the car roof and even more by the looming face a few inches from mine. I wind down the window and the man wants to know why I'm parked in his driveway.

A Fighting Chance in Wolverhampton

To Wolverhampton Civic Hall on a wet summer's evening. In my car are two other members of our group: guitarist Dave D and Fred the drummer, and we pick up Rick C on the way. Rick is a friend of our singer, John Fiddler, who we are due to meet at the concert venue. John will soon be leaving our band and in a few years will be releasing hit singles as one half of *Medicine Head*.

Tonight, though, we are not performing. We are there to see our musical heroes: Jack Bruce, Eric Clapton and Ginger

Baker – collectively *Cream*. Also on the bill is a local band called the *N' Betweens* whom I'd first come across working as a junior clerk in the Further Education and Youth Service section of the Education Department. They'd just won the Staffordshire County Council Beat Competition and we'd been sent a pile of publicity photos. They will become better known in the future as *Slade*.

My twelve-year-old Austin A30 gets us there OK. It's pretty reliable, once it gets started. It's in damp weather that getting it going in the first place is problematic. Over-use of the starter has meant that the original pull-mechanism on the dash has long since given way to a loop of coat-hanger wire. And more often than not the starting handle is needed – so much so that there's now a deep groove where it catches on the front bumper during operation. So, after parking, I light the paraffin lamp and hang it next to the engine. This should give us a fighting chance of getting home after the concert.

Up the steps and past the tall columns, we make our way to the bar. Standing one down from me is Ginger Baker. He's requesting three double vodkas and coke. He must be getting a round in, I think, but he adds, "…in the same glass." Eventually, Cream performs a brilliant set and, pumped up with the music, we run through the dogged drizzle of the adjacent car park. Fred is particularly enthused by Ginger's display of percussive dexterity and leaps onto the bonnet of a largish van before sprinting across its roof.

We pile into the A30, Dave D in the front passenger seat, Rick and Fred in the rear. There's a tap on my window. I wind it down a few inches. There's a large man in Hells Angels gear wanting to know which of us just ran over his van. His request is met with protestations of innocence, although Fred remains remarkably quiet. I look in the mirror and he seems to be shrinking into the seat. The man asks again, with noticeably more insistence this time. He has friends with him, all similarly sized and adorned. They take up positions on each side of our car which begins, quite gently, to rock. In a voice rather higher than usual, Fred suggests I "start the bloody car." There is general agreement that this is a good idea so I pull on the coat-hanger. The engine turns over but does not start. The rocking is more pronounced and there is banging on the roof, too. I try the starter again, and again. Nothing. The two teams of Angels are now competing to be the first to tip us over when one more frantic attempt bursts the car into life. Into first gear, foot down to floor and we high-rev towards an escape route. Austin A30s are not known for their acceleration, and there are other vehicles in the way, so the angry men are still in close pursuit. As I'm turning left into the road ahead I'm assessing the state of play via the rear-view mirror. There's a warning shout from my front seat passenger: I'm half on the road and half on the pavement. I swerve only just in time to avoid the looming post of a road sign and the odd startled pedestrian or two.

It's only when I judge we've driven sufficient distance for safety, that I bring the car to halt. I open the bonnet and remove the little heater, flame still flickering. It did its job, in the end, and disaster is avoided.

Learning by Mistakes

The most nervous person in the car is the guy occupying the front passenger seat. His supervisor is in the back seat, examining the examiner examining me. The man looms large in my rear-view mirror. At one stage, though, he almost disappears when without warning he falls into a prone position. My first thought is that he's died. But the examiner is instructing me to reverse the vehicle into a side road, and I'm being given a clear view so I can carry out the manoeuvre.

We all get back safely and I'm handed the piece of paper which gives me licence to roam the country's streets and highways solo. There's a nice open stretch of road ahead and I wonder how fast I could round the traffic island at the far end. One of the things you're not warned about in your driving lessons is the danger of negotiating a roundabout at top speed and without changing to a lower gear. Experiencing the peculiar sensation of travelling momentarily on two wheels, uncertain of which way up I'm likely to end, proves to be an effective way of learning this important facet of driving technique. Fortunately my car is an Austin A30, not an E-Type Jaguar.

I'm thinking about this when, two years later, my car limps home after we've been trying out a new pub. It's about twenty miles away in a part of the county I'm not well acquainted with. I drive there with Dave D and Fred and we're celebrating the last evening before the breathalyser law comes into effect. I changed my car a few weeks ago and now have a rear-engine Hillman Imp. The light front end is taking a bit of getting used to. I've heard that some owners keep a paving slab under the bonnet to aid stability but I've not yet got round to giving this a try.

Although we're now into October, the summer has been disinclined to fade; these past few weeks have been gloriously warm and everything is quite dry. This evening looks to be no exception and we're looking forward to a few pints in the pub garden. Towards closing time there's a heavy shower, but it's over by the time we climb into the car and begin the journey home. I'm paying little heed to the pretty coloured puddles where the rain has brought accumulations of oil to the top, and I barely register the sign for the sharp bend. I realise too late the need to reduce speed and slam on the brakes. The front wheels lock. The road veers to the left. We glide straight ahead. We're over the double white lines and rapidly approaching the upright signpost on the far side. Noisily, it is suddenly no longer vertical but does slow us down so that the impact with the fence and then the old oak tree is considerably reduced. Even so, Dave D's head challenges the windscreen, assisted by the hands of the rear passenger who automatically raises them as he's thrown forward by the vehicle's enforced stop.

I turn off the engine and briefly we sit in silence, coming to terms with what has just happened, but relieved that the large truck now rounding the corner was not doing so a few seconds ago. We get out to inspect the damage. It's difficult to see the detail with the headlamps shining outwards. The Imp's front and the centre of the bonnet are clearly dented and quite badly distorted, but the body doesn't appear to be restricting the wheels in any way. It's not easy, because it's straddling a ditch, but Fred and a rather dazed Dave D help me get the car back onto the road. But now the bloody thing is refusing to start. We need to push it. I explain we have to work up a decent speed so I can leap in, shove it into second and jerk my foot off the clutch pedal. After a couple of false starts, during one of which Dave D has a further brush with the vehicle when it stops abruptly, the engine comes to life.

The issue now is the gear stick. It just won't engage with any gear. From further experimental push-starts we discover that we can locate second – but only second – once the car is moving. If it stops, we're stuck. This means my two passengers will now have to jump into the car whilst it's moving. This proves especially difficult for Fred as the Hillman Imp has two doors only.

By this stage, the three of us are all pretty knackered. But at least we're on the move, albeit at no great pace. This gives us time to ponder the next set of problems. It's decided that both passengers will eject from the car – whilst it's still in motion, of course – when we get to the edge of town. This goes to plan, although it's again a harder manoeuvre for Fred. It remains for me to drive through the centre of town – and its three sets of traffic lights – without stopping. If the car comes to rest there's no-one to help with a push-start. It's well after midnight by now and the empty high street allows me to move very slowly when necessary as I attempt to anticipate the changing of the lights.

A few minutes later I'm home. Another lesson learned the hard way: new car, unfamiliar road, greasy surface and beer make a dangerous, potentially lethal, combination. And I think I now understand the reason for the breathalyser. Reluctantly, I'm a convert.

Miserable in Mevagissey

Hippies is the name given to those, mainly young, people who align themselves with some or all of the features of the 1960s counter-cultural movement that began on the west coast of the United States. These include a rejection of consumer society, a preference for communal living, support for the anti-war movement, an interest in psychedelic music and art forms, and the taking of mind-altering substances of one form or another.

Historically, the era is destined to become associated with the 'Summer of Love' of 1967. By now, hippies can be seen in many parts of the world, clearly identifiable outwardly by the wearing of beads, colourful clothing and, perhaps above all, long hair – irrespective of gender. 'True' hippies are very much a minority, but their influence in broader cultural terms – on music, fashion and the visual arts in general – is very significant.

They have also spawned the phenomenon of the 'weekend hippie' – those of us attracted by the subculture but who remain in paid employment and have not withdrawn from mainstream society. We are far more common. And so it is that four friends – Rog, Tony, Woll and myself take a holiday in Cornwall. It's a year after the hippie-inspired Summer of Love but, judging by a sign on the door of the Mevagissey pub, this small and picturesque harbourside enclave of the West Country has not yet quite caught up with the zeitgeist. *No Beatniks or Similar,* reads the sign.

'Beatnik' is a media term for those exhibiting the more superficial aspects displayed by those influenced by the *Beat Generation.* The latter was essentially an anti-materialistic literary movement which, from the late 1940s to the mid-1960s, was associated in particular with the writing of Jack Kerouac and the poetry of Allen Ginsberg. The stereotypical beatnik wore sandals and dishevelled clothes, had long, unkempt hair and, if male, sported a small beard and probably horn-rimmed glasses. The bebop modern jazz of Charlie Parker and Dizzy Gillespie provided the musical soundtrack. The beatniks can be seen as a cultural predecessor of the hippies.

As we would probably have been taken for 'Similars', rather than beatniks, we decide to press on to the next pub in the village. No notice on the door here – instead a blunt refusal to serve us and a 'request' that we take our immediate leave. Further rejections of service greet us at the remaining four pubs, including one displaying the cheerful warning: *Longhairs – do not enter and ask to be refused!*

So, thirsty – and hungry – we have no alternative but to return to the farmer's field a couple of miles away where we've pitched our tent. At least we know we'll receive a much warmer welcome at the only bar in the nearby smaller village of Gorran Haven. We'd only gone to Mevagissey for a change of scenery; the Llawnroc in Gorran Haven is our holiday local. It's here we meet up each evening with a large crowd of 'Similars' congregating from various parts of the UK. We use the open low sash window of the bar to enter and exit and on warm evenings we sit beneath the lemon tree in the garden. We listen to Keith Emerson's *The Nice* on the jukebox, drink St Austell Ales and express our disapproval of the publicans of Mevagissey.

A Principled Stance

I'm rather proud of my incorruptibility. Or is it just that I have a Samson-like aversion to haircuts? Either way, I treat with disdain my nan's attempt to bribe me to the barber's. I strongly suspect she will have been put up to this by my parents as they know what my reaction would be if they'd tried it directly. We've been here before: I was once promised £50 when I reach the age of twenty-one if I don't smoke. Well, there's no way that that's going to happen now. Too fond of the ciggies and, besides, my twenty-first is years away. It's the same amount that Nan is dangling in front of me and it's *now*. Fifty pounds is a lot of money – you can buy an awful lot of cigs with that – but I reject her offer without a moment's hesitation. I'm offended by it.

Addendum
It's not long after this that my brother receives his promise of monetary reward at age twenty-one if he's not a smoker. He never is. Over fifty years on he's still waiting for his fifty quid.

Propping Up the Bar with Paul

There are four of us on a day-trip to London. We visit the usual sights of the late 1960s – the clothes shops of the

King's Road and Carnaby Street and through the seedier parts of Soho to the heart of the music industry in Denmark Street with its guitar shops and recording studios. We see a couple of young guys openly injecting something into their arms. I've not come across that before. Tony's face pales; it makes him feel ill.

We drop into a pub for a pint and a bite to eat. Rog, Woll and Tony grab a table while I go to buy the drinks. I'm vaguely aware of a group of people entering and then standing close by continuing their conversation. The one directly to my right – our elbows touching on the polished wood of the busy bar – is wearing a sort of dusty-pink suit and dark red brogues. Quite striking, but other than that I pay him little attention. He's waiting patiently while I'm being served.

I take the tray of beers to our table. The other three are all staring in the direction I've just come from. I sit down and see that almost everyone else in the pub is doing the same. Tony says, "Didn't you notice who you were next to?" I look over but the guy is still facing the other way. It's only when he turns to his mates that I recognise Paul McCartney.

I've not been that close to a Beatle before.

Banned

We're in the park on our lunch break from work. It's a warm, calm day and a few people are playing bowls. It seems a pleasant way of passing half-an-hour so, even though none of us has played before, we decide to give it a go. We hire three sets of bowls – or woods, as I believe they're called – from the attendant. We're not sure what the little rubber mat is for until we see another player casually throwing his in front of him and then standing on it while bowling. I try to emulate the same outward flick of the wrist – but far too enthusiastically. Instead of landing on the green, the mat takes flight and is now stuck on the lower branches of an overhanging tree. It's just out of our reach. Without thinking it through, my immediate reaction is to attempt to dislodge it with one of my woods. This doesn't work but a small indentation is left in the pristine lawn following the wood's return to earth. There's an angry park attendant running towards us.

It's fairly common to hear of people being barred from places such as pubs or dance halls or restaurants because of their behaviour or appearance – indeed, I've experienced it myself. But being banned from a bowling green could be a first.

An Apt Career

I bump into an old schoolfriend – the one who was expelled just before his O-Levels for forcibly removing a radiator from the wall of the changing rooms. Neglecting to turn it off first, he had also flooded the room.

"What are you doing these days?" I ask. Without a hint of irony, he tells me he's a heating engineer.

The Scarf and the Sprouts

Bill is a work colleague and we're currently living in Coventry and attending a block-release course at Lanchester College. To fit into student life, we've each bought the obligatory blue-and-yellow college scarf. Just as with a new school satchel, a spotless, newly minted college scarf betrays your status as a fresher. I've therefore already scuffed mine up a bit. Bill takes a more staid approach to these sorts of things. Unable to persuade him verbally of the virtue of a lived-in shabbiness, I take his scarf from the chair next to mine and start to wipe the chalkboard with one end of it – for demonstration purposes. Bill is not impressed and snatches it back, promising revenge.

Later in the day, I return from a tea break to find Bill going berserk with a scarf. He's saying, "So, you like the scruffy look, do you? Well how about this?" as he switches from his manic wiping of the board to a wild dance of stamping and kicking the scarf around the floor of the room before a finale of condensation-removing applications to the classroom windows. In triumphant fashion, I'm presented with the soggy, bedraggled muffler. "There you are," he says. It's then I notice the initials inked into one end. I couldn't stop the smile. *WJ*. "This isn't mine, Bill – or, should I say 'William'?" I point out as, with all the mock humility I can muster, I return the scarf to its owner.

Although he may not yet be aware of it, Bill does get his own back, nonetheless. We share digs in a small house a couple of miles from college. Each evening we sit down with the landlady to eat the dinner she's prepared for us. I detest Brussels sprouts but make the mistake of not confessing to this on the first day in our lodgings. Mrs P now seems convinced that Bill and I both positively adore sprouts and that we could eat them until they ooze from our ears. Whatever is for dinner it is always accompanied by a vast pile of the Brussels. Fortunately for me, Bill is fine with the evil little green things. So, each evening when Mrs P interrupts her main course to add some finishing touches to the pudding in the adjacent kitchen, my sprouts are transferred to Bill's plate.

This all works satisfactorily until the evening Bill has to return for an event in his home town. There's just Mrs P and me – and the inevitable sprouts. But it's even worse than I feared. There must be twice as many as usual. "I'd forgotten Bill wouldn't be here, so you can have his share too – a special treat." There's just a small part of me that wonders if our landlady has known about our covert sprout-swapping activity all along. Or, am I paranoid in suspecting some recent collusion designed to secure Bill's revenge *in absentia*?

Middle in the Middle

The new lecturer introduces herself as "Miss Middlemiss: middle in the middle and miss at each end".

Oh Hippy Day

It begins to dawn on me even before we pile out of the car. The inside is full of smoke because we've been puffing away on the weed, apparently. We're grabbing some fresh air, I'm thinking – but, no, we're holding hands in a revolving circle and singing Ring-a-ring-o'-roses. Oh dear! After the sneezing bit we all fall down and the others dissolve into a writhing fit of giggles.

I'm really feeling out of it now. I seem to be the sole unstoned member of our band of happy little hippies dancing in the sunshine. Have I not been smoking the stuff in the right way? My observations indicate that you're supposed to take a big drag, top it up with two or three short and rapid pulls of air strained through almost closed lips, hold it all for a few seconds – and relax. I notice one or two look as if they are trying to swallow the smoke. You then pass on the crushed, hot and increasingly soggy-ended spliff to the person on your left.

Or perhaps there is something wrong with me. Am I immune to the effects of the cannabis plant, a sort of reverse allergy? I start to worry that my fellow groovy stoners will see that my kite is flying at a much lower altitude. Is that paranoia? So maybe I am blitzed after all.

It's not until later that an alternative explanation strikes me. What if the pot we'd been smoking was part of a duff, or very weak, batch and the others were each feeling no more than I was but not wanting to admit it (as I didn't), or were desperately willing it to work (ditto for me). After all, I had joined in the silly prancing about...

There'd been six of us in the car that day. At least two of them are now widening their field of experimentation, following up each tale they hear of everyday products (and produce) capable of producing highs – however risky or ludicrous it seems to the rest of us. One swears by the hallucinatory effects he gets from over-dosing on Marzine travel-sickness tablets; another has joined a group specialising in the abuse of a certain brand of cough mixture. Local greengrocers must be pleased with a recent upturn in their banana sales as rituals develop around their preparation. The fruit is peeled and the skins are oven-baked (I don't know about the timing or the gas mark). Their inner surfaces are then scraped and added to roll-ups which are smoked. Subsequently the inside may be eaten to quell an attack of the munchies (but this is optional). All bollocks, of course, but I suppose everyone should have a hobby.

There's a lurking threat, an undertow, emerging as the initial innocence of hippiedom is becoming usurped by more sinister developments. There are rumours that some on the fringes of our, admittedly quite wide, circle of friends and acquaintances are now into regular use of harder drugs. This suggests that the small-time suppliers of cannabis in our barely medium-sized town are already being pushed out by the big boys of the drug-supply gangs from outside.

I and most of my friends are steering clear. For my part, I'd like to say it's because I have more sense, but I suspect it's more to do with fear.

Ello, Ello, Ello!

For the third time tonight I'm stopped by the police on my four-mile walk home from Anne's. For the third time a panda car pulls up a few yards ahead. The lone occupant leans over to the passenger side, winds down the window and the usual questions begin. What is your name? Where do you live? Where are you going? Where have you been? Why are you out at this time of night?

I tell the constable it's the third time tonight this has happened and I'm getting tired of answering these questions. He says he's stopped me because I look... But his sentence hangs in the air. You look... Again there's a pause. He seems to be searching for a word, but it just won't come to him. Eventually he gives up and with a dismissive wave of the hand sends me on my way.

I continue my walk but within a minute the car pulls alongside me with the window still down. "Suspicious," he yells triumphantly from the driver's seat, "You looked suspicious." And with that, he revs off.

Barely have I finished chuckling to myself when yet another police car draws to a halt. This time I'm ready to be awkward and brace myself for an argument. I bend down to peer into the vehicle. The first 'Wh' escapes from his lips but nothing immediately follows except for looks of mutual surprise. I know you. And I know you. I haven't seen him for a while but we used to meet quite regularly and each time money would change hands.

Where're you off to?

On my way home.

Hop in. I'll give you a lift.

Thanks.

On the way, he's telling me about how he packed in his boring job at the bank to join the police force. It's not bad, he says, and you get to drive around in one of these cars. He drops me off at the bottom of my road – in case nosey neighbours are wondering why you are in a police car, he says. That's considerate of him, although I doubt any of them would be awake at 2.30 in the morning.

Something to Meditate on

Om is variously described as the foundation or supreme power of the universe, or the universe's primal sound vibration. As such it is the most sacred mantra in Hinduism and Tibetan Buddhism. Interest in aspects of Eastern religions and practices, including types of meditation, has been growing in the West, particularly since the visit of the Beatles earlier this year to the Maharishi Mahesh at his Indian retreat. After their return, the Beatles record the John Lennon song *Across The Universe* in which the *om* mantra is repeatedly intoned.

We're idling the time away over the Chase, between Milford and Brocton, and chatting to an acquaintance. He tells us that in order meditate successfully, you don't have to use *om*. It doesn't even need to be a single word or sound. It can, he says, be a few random words strung together. He explains that his own personal mantra consists of four unconnected words which he repeats over and again to himself in fairly rapid succession.

"Why don't we all try it now?" he suggests, as with a stick he writes out the words in the sand. Against my better judgement, I join in as we chant in unison:

Whale
Oil
Beef
Hooked

Don't Delay

After attending an (unsuccessful) job interview with the London Borough of Hillingdon, I receive repayment of my expenses through the post. The typed note on the accompanying compliment slip reads: "Please pass this cheque for payment as soon as possible," and is signed "B. Quick, Borough Treasurer".

Ello, Ello, Again

My early hours trek home is not interrupted until I'm on the final stretch of the walk. As usual, it's a police panda car. This policeman is new to me and is particularly offensive in his questioning. In response, I'm even less co-operative than normal and refuse to answer most of his questions. He tells me to get into the car. I ask if I am being arrested because if not, I can't be compelled to do so. He just repeats his order, making it very clear that, in practice, I have little choice. He's a lot bigger than I am and he's also the one with the truncheon.

Once in the vehicle, the questioning continues as does my unwillingness to respond in the way he wants. I've been reading up on my legal rights in these situations and

I know that most of what he's telling me is bullshit. His exasperation and impatience ups a level when I impart this information to him.

"Right," he says, "I'm taking you down to the station." He U-turns and we're heading back into town.

"Would that be the railway station or the bus station?" I enquire.

My attempt at humour is not appreciated. "I'm taking you in," he snarls.

"Why?"

"Because you are not answering my questions."

"Am I being arrested?"

"I'm taking you back for questioning."

I don't want to go. I ask him to stop and let me out. He continues to drive. I tell him he's going to look stupid when he takes me in and his Desk Sergeant asks him why I'm there. He doesn't reply but I can see his mind ticking over. Just round the corner from the station, he stops the car and instructs me to get out.

"I'm not getting out here. You've taken me more than two miles in the opposite direction from where I was going. Take me into the station: I want to make a complaint of unlawful arrest."

He gets out of the car and walks slowly round to my side, looking up and down the street. There's not a soul about. He opens the door and assists me out of the seat – quite quickly. If I know what's good for me I'll now fuck off home quietly, I'm told. "You do understand, don't you?"

I start on the long walk home.

A Treat on my Twenty-first

The message comes down the line. The boss wants to see me. How nice – he must have consulted the file, seen that it's my twenty-first birthday and wants to pass on his good wishes. Or perhaps a pay-rise is in the offing?

So, it's with an appropriately expectant air that I enter the man's office. His face seems a little stern, given the occasion, and I'm not invited to sit.

"I've received a complaint."

This throws me and I respond only with a question-mark expression.

"It's about your behaviour in town last Friday lunch-time. Apparently you were seen fighting in the street. Does that ring any bells?"

Of course it bloody does. It's not every day you get attacked in the main street by a total stranger who stops you and tells you to get a haircut before landing a right hook on the side of your face. It comes completely out of the blue and I'm momentarily dazed, in any case, by the severity of the blow. I become aware though that this nutter is about to take a second swing at me and I just have time to shove him out of the way. He stumbles backwards, prevented from falling only by the shop window of Woodall's the drapers. For a moment I think he is going straight through the large sheet of plate glass – and get a flash of his smart white mac splattered with blood – but it just rattles alarmingly. His flailing left arm releases a shopping bag I'd not noticed. A few items of fruit and a French stick distribute themselves among the feet of shoppers on the busy pavement. As he gets back properly onto his pins, his eyes tell me he's gearing up for another go so I stay up close trying to out-glare him. Someone steps between us, telling us both to stop and calm down. It's only then I'm conscious of the smallish but curious crowd that has gathered. There's a lot of staring and some tutting, too.

Other than taking an obvious dislike to my hair, I've no idea why this man has physically assaulted me.

Judging by his clean-cut, 'respectable' appearance (possibly middle-ranking management of some sort) and his age (probably mid– to late-thirties), I wouldn't have expected it. Back at work, Mrs Brassington sees I'm shaken. Her husband is a police inspector and she urges me to report the incident immediately. But I don't. I just want to forget about it.

I explain most of this to my boss, emphasising I acted only and entirely in self-defence. "Sometimes," he intones, "one has to turn the other cheek." Sod that for a game of soldiers, I think, the man had already half-busted my left one. Then I remember the boss is a churchgoer (and probably a member of the local lodge, as well). God save us from pious bloody Christians.

I suppose what I'm then treated to is a formal verbal warning, although the phrase isn't used. "Happy birthday," I say to myself on the way out. Well, I'm not going to hear it from the boss today, am I.

Walking on the Moon/It's All Over Now

Like Lanny Budd in the Upton Sinclair series of novels, some people have the knack of being in the right place at the right time. That perfect intersection of great events and personal history seems to evade me, however. A date arranged with a new girlfriend without checking the calendar results in my sacrificing England's famous World Cup final victory. *They think it's all over…* it is by the time I arrive home that late Saturday afternoon.

Three years on and I'm all set up to watch the first ever moonwalk on our black-and-white TV. Reports had already come in about the safe landing of the Eagle just after 8.15. But there's not a great deal to see as the hours pass. Mum has gone up to bed a while ago. Dad sticks with it until about 2.00 am. An accumulation of late nights is catching up on me and I'm nodding a bit but I hear, rather than see, that the hatch of the module has opened so it shouldn't be long now.

"You still up then?" Mum is setting the table for breakfast. The screen is blank. According to the radio, Neil and Buzz returned safely to the landing craft hours ago. It's all over: the small step and the giant leap, the bouncing across the surface, the inevitable planting of the American flag and the unveiling of the plaque signed by President Nixon. Missed it all.

And I'm due at work in an hour's time.

On the Move?

In hospital for the extraction of problematic wisdom teeth.

Nurse: "Have you moved?"

Me: "No. I've been here since yesterday."

Nurse: "Have you movement?"

Me: "Oh, yes. I'm just here for the teeth."

Nurse: "Do you move today?"

Me: "Only to the operating theatre then I expect I'll be returning here."

This seems an odd line of questioning. Surely, as the nurse she would know the answers already? But she is looking even more puzzled than I am. She tries a different tack.

Nurse: "Have you evacuation?"

I can't think of how to reply other than to say I don't think this has happened since the war.

The confusion has shifted a level and the nurse is seeking advice from a colleague on the far side of the ward, she returns with a smile.

Nurse: "Have your bowels moved today?"

Ah!

Tragic Outcomes

It's a summer evening and I've arranged to meet Jack in the bar at the back of the old hotel near the town centre. I find him in conversation with a somewhat older man I've not seen before. Jack is looking uneasy and seems relieved to see me. I join them at the table and I'm introduced to James, a slightly built yet wiry-looking guy with an instant aura of menace. James offers a heavily but inexpertly tattooed hand, his arm extending only from the elbow, which remains close to his body. I reach across to take it and am immediately grasped in the most achingly crushing grip imaginable. Instead of the up-and-down movement of the conventional handshake, I'm pulled further across the table so I'm forced to look into a pair of unblinking penetratingly blue eyes from a distance of a few inches. I'm still fearing for the future of my right hand: if not for the general hubbub of the bar, I'm sure I'd hear the bones cracking and scraping as the clench moves to a level I didn't think possible. But it's the eyes which are commanding attention. The pupils are dilated but the vivid blueness surrounding the black is clear and deep.

This is scary. The man is saying something to me. I hear aggression but I can't find a way through the very strong accent. Jack is looking even more worried, his eyes flicking from side-to-side, but he starts to translate.

"He's asking if you have drugs."

"Sorry, James, I don't have any."

"Money, then."

"I just have my bus fare home," I blurt out implausibly.

For some reason, my hand is released. There's a bit of a hiatus during which Jack squeezes past me mumbling he's just going to the Gents'. Things are really uncomfortable now. James, sporadically, is still talking at me. I'm only making out the occasional word but to my ears they're all replete with impending danger. And the longer Jack is away the more alarming they become. Those eyes never leave me.

"I'll just see what's keeping Jack." I'm sure my voice is higher than normal; I don't feel in control of it.

As I head towards the outside toilet I'm aware James is close behind. As soon as I'm through the door and into the little courtyard with the entrance to the toilets ahead, he's in front of me. I'm backing almost to the old brick wall. There's no mistaking the threats now even if their precise nature continues to elude me. But then there's the gesture and the deep, unfeeling stare that accompanies it. His left hand is drawn in a slow, slicing movement against his own throat while the other, the one that greeted me so emphatically a few minutes ago, reaches inside his dark denim jacket.

Over his shoulder I glimpse Jack emerging from the Gents'. He rapidly takes in the scene.

"Run! *bloody run!*"

I obey and somehow my jelly legs manage to keep up with Jack as he sprints through the hotel car park and we turn onto Mill Street. It's amazing what the image of a razor-wielding, drug-fuelled maniac in frenzied pursuit can do for one's powers of acceleration. Whether or not the man is actually giving chase is not the point. In calm retrospect, he probably isn't. But we don't look behind to check. In fact we don't stop running until we're more than half a mile and many streets away.

Breath caught and feeling safer, Jack gives me the background. He says he knows the man – he lives not far from him – and something of his history. Born in a Gorbals tenement, James and his siblings were not so much raised as left to fend for themselves from a very young age. Instead of beds, as infants they apparently slept in drawers from an old chest. In the 1930s this was not unheard of among poor families. Presumably less common was the practice adopted in James' household of re-inserting the occupied drawers into the chest for the night.

I don't interrupt Jack to ask how he knows these details for I'm already drawn in and want to hear more. There seems almost an inevitability about the next part. James spends much of his childhood in a variety of institutions. Once he reaches the required age, these are soon of the custodial kind and he spends more of his adult years inside prison than out.

According to Jack, he's recently been charged with doing to a complete stranger what a few minutes ago he'd threatened to do to me. Jesus! And earlier this evening, the man had confided in Jack his ambition to commit mass murder. Oh! Bloody hell; this gets worse. We decide it will be wise, for a while, to keep away from the town centre in the evenings. Until things die down, I say, before I recognise the unfortunate choice of word. Although Jack cannot hope for the same, given his prior acquaintance with the man, I'm thinking that, after a period of time perhaps James won't even remember me should our paths cross again.

But he does. It's a few weeks later on a crowded Saturday afternoon and I'm walking through the town with Anne. Also with a female companion, and coming towards me, is James. Our eyes lock and those eyes... those eyes are giving me the same message as before. As I veer into the narrow entry running alongside Boots, pulling Anne with me, do

I glimpse that hand about to start a repeat of that gesture? This time, after a few yards, I do look behind. He's gone. Perhaps the presence of his friend or of too many shoppers has been a constraint.

Jack had thought we shouldn't worry too much in any case since it won't be long before the man is back inside. And he's right. There's a guy in a serious condition in hospital. He has life-changing head injuries. The rumour is he's a relative of James and the two had been drinking all day at a local club. The following morning the emergency services receive a call from James reporting that he's found an unconscious man in his living room. It turns out he's been lying there all night after being attacked with a variety of weapons, including a golf club and an axe. James had then decided to go to bed, leaving his drinking companion on the floor. The upshot is that while the victim is just about hanging on to life, James is now back in prison charged with attempted murder. And visits to the venues of the town centre should be that bit safer, at least for now.

But things will get worse... much worse. Several years later, I'm reading a press report of a court case. I recognise the man in the photograph. He's looking noticeably older and the chilling stare is gone or is not captured. He's in a wheelchair. Two bodies had been discovered at his home and this is why the man is up before the judge and jury of the Crown Court. It seems that James' partner had recently left, taking their two children with her. James had been granted access, however, and – believing his children were not being properly looked after – had notified the authorities accordingly. I am told later that social workers were aware of the situation but that a planned visit to the mother was not considered urgent. During the times that James was responsible for the children he seemed to be coping well and there was a genuine bond between the kids and their father. It seems, however, that James thought he was going to lose them. He drowned the two children in the bath before carrying them back to their room and returning them to bed. He then made an unsuccessful attempt to take his own life.

While on remand he leaps from a high window of a hospital in a second suicide attempt – and his back is broken.

Three lives wasted. Two of them barely begun.

Cows

I find cows to be unpredictable animals. They can be rather frightening, especially when acting collectively.

I'm walking the footpath between the fields at the top of our road and see a dozen or so Guernseys moving in rapid, un-cattle-like fashion towards the far side. The reason soon becomes clear. They are being chased by someone's pet dog irresponsibly let off its lead. Cows and dog disappear over the brow of a hill. I'm just about to move off when the dog reappears, ears flat and tail between legs, running like the clappers back to its owner – closely followed by the annoyed Guernseys. I didn't see the point at which the cows, presumably as one, turned – but I'd have loved to.

This episode comes a few weeks after Anne and I had spent an afternoon just a mile or two away in the grounds of Shugborough Hall. Cows are dotted around across the river and the occasional lowing carries easily across the wide, treeless fields. I can do a passable imitation of a mooing cow so I return a few calls from my side of the water. After a while of these exchanges, the cattle interrupt their grazing and start to walk in our direction. This is odd, but not too unnerving – until the lead cow does not stop at the river bank but continues into the water, followed by another... and another. It's like the approaching undead in a horror movie. At this point, Anne and I turn tail and flee back through the narrow woodland area to the safety of the Hall gardens. I promise to confine my bovine impressions to safer environs in future.

Move On Up

Bookings is what we called them whenever our old group was engaged to play a venue. Now I keep seeing references to *gigs* and *gigging* in the music press. I bump into an old musician acquaintance and decide to try out the new vocab. It's not until I've already begun to ask the question that I realize I've never heard the word spoken. Is the initial *g* a hard or soft one? An immediate decision is called for.

'Played any good jigs lately?'

Wrong choice.

Am I becoming out of touch? Stale? I get bored at work and resent how it steals my time. I'm still living at home and Anne at hers. Our choices of activity are limited and the places we visit are becoming routine. Life is jogging along when we still want to run. My teenage years might officially be over and the decade has ended, but I'm not prepared to give up on all that the 1950s promised and the 60s have started to deliver. The pyramids have broken through the slate days to sparkle in the sunshine.

Yet for the sunny days to continue things must change. It's time to move on up. But to what? And to where?

Addendum

A Few Family Words and Sayings

I suppose most families come out with certain phrases and ways of expressing things, some common within your own district or region, some connected more closely with a particular generation, and so on. These are (some frequently, some less so) heard within my own family.

All around the Wrekin – widely used in the counties of and adjacent to the West Midlands, it refers to the practice of taking too long to say or explain something. The Wrekin is a hill in Shropshire which on a clear day can be seen from high points in the Stafford area. My favourite viewing position for the Wrekin is by the gravel pits at Brocton. I could wax lyrical on the beauties of the Wrekin but this would risk the phrase being applied to me.

You'll get a pig's foot growing on the end of it – this easily disputable threat is meant to be a parental warning of the dangers of nose-picking. It's not entirely clear if the foot will extend from the nose or the finger.

They don't study you, do they? – the words 'study' and 'do' are accentuated. Used in particular by my nan if she thinks any of her grandchildren are insufficiently considerate of her. Intended for use within their earshot, despite ostensibly directed at a third person (usually the other nan).

Nesh – feeling the cold too easily, as in the response to your complaint that the inside of your bedroom window is all frosted-up: "Aaah, you're nesh; just enjoy the pretty patterns Jack Frost has drawn for you."

Blood's thicker than water – this commonly used phrase, implying that family ties are closer than others, tends to be used by my parents in a resigned, even exasperated, fashion – usually prefaced by the words 'I suppose' – hinting that I wouldn't be worth bothering with if I wasn't closely related to them.

Mardy arse – applied to anyone deploying petulant behaviour or indulging in the sulks.

You look like you've lost a shilling and found sixpence – the post-decimalisation equivalent 'lost 5p and found 2.5p', although making the saying self-explanatory for younger generations, would lose some of the punch of the original.

...a face like a smacked bum – the posher version of 'you've a face like a slapped arse', i.e. you're looking exceedingly miserable.

Skwitch or *squitch* – head hair so thick and unruly that you can 'barely drag a comb through it'.

Acknowledgements

Memory can be a slippery creature. Yet, allowing for its nefarious box of tricks – including the conflation of two or more episodes or the transposition of locations or people – I've been surprised at how many of my memories have since received independent corroboration from people I knew at the time. I'd assumed that stories I've been telling for years must have received many coatings of embellishment. I'd begun to suspect that some might even be inventions. It's been encouraging to discover that even the smallest details have quite often coincided when old friends or renewed acquaintances have been asked to recall particular occurrences or characters. Given the geographical mobility of my baby-boom generation, most of these recollections have taken place via social media or through the far slower but more satisfying form of letter-writing. This is all to the better, I think, because the dangers of the collective enhancement of stories shared repeatedly among friends who grow old in each other's company is largely avoided.

Additionally, there is what to me and others of my age is still the revelatory experience of being able to fact-check many aspects of time, place and societal events almost instantly without leaving our chairs. A generation of active, post-war but pre-TV kids is transformed into a bunch of sedentary, yet extremely knowledgeable, old sods.

So, I am grateful to all the old sods who have helped, in one way or another, with the reconstruction of my memories. In some cases this has led to the rekindling of friendships unkindled for many decades. Special thanks are due to John Tully with whom such a friendship has been so happily and rewardingly restored after a separation of more than 10,000 miles and fifty years. I'm grateful to Rob Fiddy for his encouragingly shrewd observations at an early stage in the project. Barry, John and Dave have also kindly checked drafts of particular sections. As usual, I'm indebted to Anne. The final versions of many of the pieces have benefited greatly from her input and she has also produced the lovely (if uncomfortably pithy) line drawings. Above all, though, it is her continuing and constructive support that means the most.

And to my parents who gave me the best start in life it was possible for them to give – my eternal gratitude, and apologies.